Raspberry Pi

Twitter Bot, Unique mark Sensor, Ball Tracking
Robot, Plex Media Server, GPIO Pins utilizing
Telegram App, Oscilloscope etc,..

Raspberry Pi - Twitter Bot, Unique mark Sensor, Ball Tracking Robot, Plex Media Server, GPIO Pins utilizing Telegram App, Oscilloscope etc,.

CONTENTS

ACKNOWLEDGMENTS

The writer might want to recognize the diligent work of the article group in assembling this book. He might likewise want to recognize the diligent work of the Raspberry Pi Foundation and the Arduino bunch for assembling items and networks that help to make the Internet of Things increasingly open to the overall population. Yahoo for the democratization of innovation!

INTRODUCTION

The Internet of Things (IOT) is a perplexing idea comprised of numerous PCs and numerous correspondence ways. Some IOT gadgets are associated with the Internet and some are most certainly not. Some IOT gadgets structure swarms that convey among themselves. Some are intended for a solitary reason, while some are increasingly universally useful PCs. This book is intended to demonstrate to you the IOT from the back to front. By structure IOT gadgets, the per user will comprehend the essential ideas and will almost certainly develop utilizing the rudiments to make his or her very own IOT applications. These included ventures will tell the per user the best way to assemble their very own IOT ventures and to develop the models appeared. The significance of Computer Security in IOT gadgets is additionally talked about and different systems for protecting the IOT from unapproved clients or programmers. The most significant takeaway from this book is in structure the tasks yourself.

1. RASPBERRY PI BASED OSCILLOSCOPE

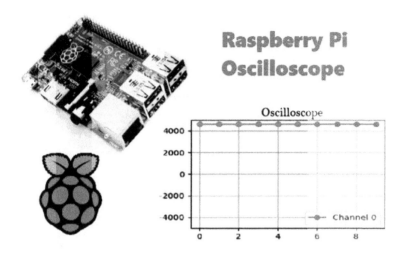

Hey folks, welcome to the present post. One of the most intriguing thing about being a creator is realizing how to create improvised apparatuses, you will never stall out taking a shot at any undertaking when you have that sort of adaptability. So Today, I will share how to construct a Raspberry Pi based stopgap variant of one of the most significant apparatuses in Electrical/Electronics building; The Oscilloscope.

The oscilloscope is an electronic test instrument that permits the representation and perception of changing sign voltages, for the most part as a 2 dimensional plot with at least one sign plotted against time. The present venture will try to imitate the sign perception capacities of the oscilloscope utilizing the Raspberry Pi and a simple to advanced converter module.

Project Flow:

Duplicating the sign perception of the oscilloscope utilizing the Raspberry Pi will require the accompanying advances;

1. Perform Digital to simple transformation of the Input sign

2. Set up the subsequent information for portrayal

3. Plot the information on a live time chart

An improved square outline for this task would resemble the chart beneath.

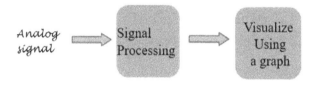

Project Requirements

The prerequisite for this task can be grouped into two:

- Programming Requirements
- Equipment Requirements

Equipment necessities

To assemble this task, the accompanying segments/

part are required;

- Raspberry pi 2 (or some other model)
- LAN/Ethernet Cable
- 8 or 16GB Secure Digital Card
- ADS1115 ADC
- Power Supply or USB link
- 10k or 1k resistor
- LDR (Optional as its implied for test)
- Breadboard
- Jumper wires
- Screen or some other method for seeing the pi's Desktop(VNC comprehensive)

Programming Requirements

The product prerequisites for this task are fundamentally the python modules (matplotlib and drawnow) that will be utilized for information perception and the Adafruit module for interfacing with the ADS1115 ADC chip. I will tell the best way to introduce these modules on the Raspberry Pi as we continue.

While this instructional exercise will work independent of the raspberry pi OS utilized, I will utilize the Raspberry Pi stretch OS and I will expect you know about setting up the Raspberry Pi with the

Raspbian stretch OS, and you know how to SSH into the raspberry pi utilizing a terminal programming like putty. In the event that you have problem with any of this, there are huge amounts of Raspberry Pi Tutorials on this site can help.

With all the equipment segments set up, we should make the schematics and interface the parts together.

Circuit Diagram:

To change over the simple information sign to computerized signals which can be pictured with the Raspberry Pi, we will utilize the ADS1115 ADC chip. This chip becomes significant on the grounds that the Raspberry Pi, not at all like Arduino and most smaller scale controllers, doesn't have an on-board simple to computerized converter(ADC). While we could have utilized any raspberry pi perfect ADC chip, I lean toward this chip because of its high resolution(16bits) and its very much recorded datasheet and use guidelines by Adafruit. You can likewise check our Raspberry Pi ADC instructional exercise to become familiar with it.

The ADC is an I2C based gadget and ought to be associated with the Raspberry Pi as appeared in the schematics underneath.

For lucidity, the stick association between the two segments is additionally portrayed beneath.

11

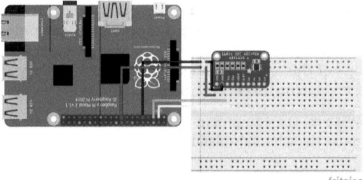

fritzing

ADS1115 and Raspberry Pi Connections:

VDD - 3.3v

GND - GND

SDA - SDA

SCL - SCL

With the associations all done, control up your pi and continue to introduce the conditions referenced beneath.

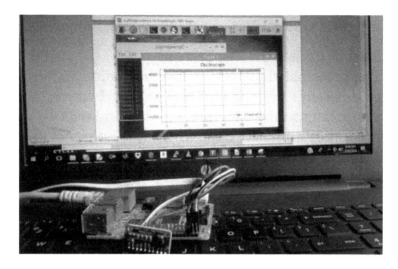

Install Dependencies for Raspberry Pi Oscilloscope:

Before we start composing the python content to pull information from the ADC and plot it on a live diagram, we have to empower the I2C correspondence interface of the raspberry pi and introduce the product prerequisites that were referenced before. This will be done in underneath steps so its simple to pursue:

Stage 1: Enable Raspberry Pi I2C interface

To empower the I2C, from the terminal, run;

sudo raspi-config

At the point when the design boards open, select

interface alternatives, select I2C and snap empower.

Stage 2: Update the Raspberry pi

The principal thing I do before beginning any venture is refreshing the Pi. Through this, I am certain everything on the OS is forward-thinking and I won't encounter similarity issue with any most recent programming I decide to introduce on the Pi. To do this, run underneath two directions:

```
sudo apt-get update

sudo apt-get upgrade
```

Stage 3: Install the Adafruit ADS1115 library for ADC

With the update done, we are currently prepared to introduce the conditions beginning with the Adafruit python module for the ADS115 chip. Guarantee you are in the Raspberry Pi home registry by running;

```
cd ~
```

at that point introduce the construct basics by running;

```
sudo apt-get install build-essential python-dev
python-smbus git
```

Next, clone the Adafruit git organizer for the library by running;

```
git     clone     https://github.com/adafruit/
Adafruit_Python_ADS1x15.git
```

Change into the cloned document's registry and run the arrangement record;

```
cd Adafruit_Python_ADS1x1z

sudo python setup.py install
```

After establishment, your screen should resemble the picture underneath.

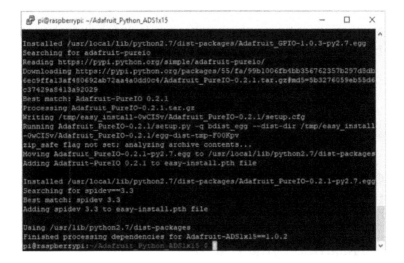

Stage 4: Test the library and 12C correspondence.

Before we continue with the remainder of the under-taking, it is critical to test the library and guarantee the ADC can speak with the raspberry pi over I2C. To do this we will utilize a model content that accompanies the library.

While still in the Adafruit_Python_ADS1x15 organizer, change registry to the models catalog by running;

```
cd examples
```

Next, run the sampletest.py model which shows the estimation of the four directs on the ADC in a forbidden structure.

Run the model utilizing:

python simpletest.py

In case the I2C module is empowered and associations great, you should consider the to be as appeared in the picture beneath.

In the event that a mistake happens, check to guarantee the ADC is all around associated with the PI and I2C correspondence is empowered on the Pi.

Stage 5: Install Matplotlib

To picture the information we have to introduce the matplotlib module which is utilized to plot all sort of diagrams in python. This should be possible by running;

sudo apt-get install python-matplotlib

You must view a result like the picture beneath.

Step6: Install the Drawnow python module

Ultimately, we have to introduce the drawnow python module. This module encourages us give live updates to the information plot.

We will introduce drawnow through the python bundle installer; pip, so we have to guarantee it is introduced. This should be possible by running;

sudo apt-get install python-pip

We would then be able to utilize pip to introduce the drawnow bundle by running:

sudo pip install drawnow

You ought to get a result like the picture underneath in case of running it.

With every conditions introduced, we are presently prepared to compose the code.

Python Code for Raspberry Pi Oscilloscope:

The python code for this Pi Oscilloscope is genuinely basic particularly in the event that you know about the python matplotlib module. Before demonstrating us the entire code, I will attempt to break it into part and clarify what each piece of the code is doing so you can have enough information to stretch out the code to accomplish more stuffs.

At this stage it is critical to change to a screen or utilize the VNC watcher, anything through which you can see your Raspberry Pi's work area, as the diagram being plotted won't appear on the terminal.

With the screen as the interface open another python

document. You can consider it any name you need, however I will call it scope.py.

```
sudo nano scope.py
```

With the record made, the principal thing we do is import the modules we will utilize;

```
import time

import matplotlib.pyplot as plt

from drawnow import *

import Adafruit_ADS1x15
```

Next, we make a case of the ADS1x15 library indicating the ADS1115 ADC

```
adc = Adafruit_ADS1x15.ADS1115()
```

Next, we set the increase of the ADC. There are various scopes of increase and ought to be picked dependent on the voltage you are expecting at the contribution of the ADC. For this instructional exercise, we are evaluating a 0 - 4.09v so we will utilize an increase of 1. For more information on gain you can check the

ADS1015/ADS1115 datasheet.

```
GAIN = 1
```

Next, we have to make the exhibit factors that will be utilized to store the information to be plotted and another to fill in as tally.

```
Val = [ ]

cnt = 0
```

Next, we make know our goals of making the plot intelligent referred to empower us plot the information live.

```
plt.ion()
```

Next, we start ceaseless ADC change determining the ADC channel, for this situation, channel 0 and we additionally indicate the increase.

It should be noticed that all the four ADC channels on the ADS1115 can be perused simultaneously, however 1 channel is sufficient for this showing.

```
adc.start_adc(0, gain=GAIN)
```

Next we make a capacity def makeFig, to make and set the properties of the chart which will hold our live plot. We above all else set the breaking points of the y-hub utilizing ylim, after which we input the title of the plot, and the name before we indicate the information that will be plotted and its plot style and shading utilizing plt.plot(). We can likewise express the channel (as channel 0 was expressed) so we can distinguish each sign when the four channels of the ADC are being utilized. plt.legend is utilized to determine where we need the data about that signal(e.g Channel 0) showed on the figure.

```
plt.ylim(-5000,5000)

plt.title('Osciloscope')

plt.grid(True)

plt.ylabel('ADC outputs')

plt.plot(val, 'ro-', label='lux')

plt.legend(loc='lower right')
```

Next we compose the while circle which will be utilized always read information from the ADC and update the plot as needs be.

The principal thing we do is perused the ADC change esteem

```
value = adc.get_last_result()
```

Next we print the incentive on the terminal just to give us another method for affirming the plotted information. We hold up a couple of moments subsequent to printing then we annex the information to the rundown (val) made to store the information for that channel.

```
print('Channel 0: {0}'.format(value))

time.sleep(0.5)

val.append(int(value))
```

We at that point call drawnow to refresh the plot.

```
drawnow(makeFig)
```

To guarantee the most recent information is what is accessible on the plot, we erase the information at list 0 after each 50 information checks.

```
cnt = cnt+1

if(cnt>50):

val.pop(0)
```

There's nothing more to it!

The total Python code is given toward the finish of this instructional exercise.

Raspberry Pi Oscilloscope in Action:

Duplicate the total python code and glue in the python record we made before, recall that we will require a screen to see the plot so the entirety of this ought to be finished by either VNC or with an associated screen or screen.

Spare the code and run utilizing;

```
sudo python scope.py
```

In case you utilized an alternate name other than scope.py, remember to change this to coordinate.

Following a couple of moments, you should view the ADC information being imprinted on the terminal. Every so often you may get an admonition from matplotlib (as appeared in the picture beneath) which ought to be smothered however it doesn't influence the information being shown or the plot in any case. To stifle the notice in any case, the accompanying lines of code can be included after the import lines in our code.

Import warnings

import matplotlib.cbook

warnings.filterwarnings("ignore", category=matplotlib.cbook.mplDeprecation)

```
pi@raspberrypi:~ $ sudo nano scope.py
pi@raspberrypi:~ $ sudo python scope.py
Reading ADS1x15 channel 0
Channel 0: 4618
/usr/lib/python2.7/dist-packages/matplotlib/backend
plotlibDeprecationWarning: Using default event loop
cific to this GUI is implemented
  warnings.warn(str, mplDeprecation)
Channel 0: 4615
Channel 0: 4616
Channel 0: 4615
Channel 0: 4614
Channel 0: 4613
Channel 0: 4614
```

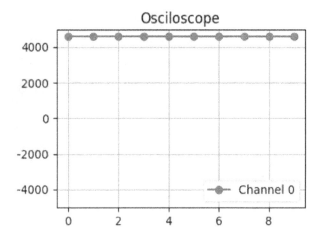

That is it for this instructional exercise folks, to completely test your oscilloscope, you can interface a simple gadget like a potentiometer to a channel on the ADC as well as you must view the information change with each turn of the potentiometer. Or then again you can include Sine wave or square wave to test the yield.

Much obliged for perusing, in case you have any question(s) or something you will like me to include, simply leave me a remark.

Till next time, Keep making!

Code

```
import time
import matplotlib.pyplot as plt
#import numpy
from drawnow import *
```

```
# Import the ADS1x15 module.
import Adafruit_ADS1x15
# Create an ADS1115 ADC (16-bit) instance.
adc = Adafruit_ADS1x15.ADS1115()
GAIN = 1
val = [ ]
cnt = 0
plt.ion()
# Start continuous ADC conversions on channel 0
using the previous gain value.
adc.start_adc(0, gain=GAIN)
print('Reading ADS1x15 channel 0')
#create the figure function
def makeFig():
  plt.ylim(-5000,5000)
  plt.title('Osciloscope')
  plt.grid(True)
  plt.ylabel('ADC outputs')
  plt.plot(val, 'ro-', label='Channel 0')
  plt.legend(loc='lower right')
while (True):
   # Read the last ADC conversion value and print it
out.
  value = adc.get_last_result()
  print('Channel 0: {0}'.format(value))
  # Sleep for half a second.
  time.sleep(0.5)
  val.append(int(value))
  drawnow(makeFig)
  plt.pause(.000001)
```

```
cnt = cnt + 1
if(cnt > 50):
  val.pop(0)
```

◆ ◆ ◆

2. SETTING UP WIRELESS ACCESS POINT UTILIZING RASPBERRY PI

Hello folks, today I will tell the best way to transform the Raspberry Pi into a remote passage to which different gadgets can associate with, fundamentally we are transforming the raspberry pi into a remote "switch". As a little something extra, I will likewise be telling us the best way to arrangement the remote passage made to give (share) web get to to(with) associated gadgets. So we should start making Wi-Fi Hotspot with Raspberry Pi.

Required Components:

The accompanying segments will be expected to set up a raspberry pi as a remote passageway:

- Raspberry Pi 2
- 8GB SD card
- WiFi USB dongle
- Ethernet cable
- Power supply for the Pi.
- Monitor (optional)
- Keyboard (optional)
- Mouse (optional)

While the Raspberry Pi 3 and Pi zero are generally accessible and could have been utilized, for this instructional exercise, I will utilize the Raspberry Pi 2 in light of the fact that my Pi3 is at present occupied with playing out some overwhelming PC vision related assignment, which I plan to partake in an instructional exercise here soon. This method in any case, likewise works for the pi 3 and should (note the accentuation) additionally work for the Raspberry Pi zero W. When utilizing the Raspberry Pi 3 or the Zero W there won't be a requirement for an outer Wi-Fi module as these two sheets as of now have Wi-Fi ready.

To characterize the objectives of this instructional exercise all the more complicatedly, we will enable our Raspberry Pi to fill in as a remote passage and to accomplish this, we should introduce and arrangement a product that furnishes the raspberry pi with this usefulness alongside a DHCP server programming to give a system address to the gadgets which will be associated with the passageway. To fulfill this product prerequisite, we will utilize the dnsmasq and the hostapd virtual products.

This instructional exercise will be founded on the Raspbian stretch OS, so to continue obviously, I will expect you know about setting up the Raspberry Pi with the Raspbian stretch OS, and you know how to SSH into the raspberry pi utilizing a terminal programming like putty. On the off chance that you have issues with any of this, there are huge amounts of Raspberry Pi Tutorials on this site can help.

Steps for Setting up Raspberry Pi as Wireless Access Point:

By following the accompanying key advances, in a steady progression, we will have the option to arrangement the raspberry pi as a remote passageway. It ought to be noticed that some remote USB dongle wont work in AP mode yet in the wake of attempting this dongle and it worked, I am enticed to state 5 out of 8 dongles will work.

Stage 1: Update the Pi

Not surprisingly, we update the raspberry pi to guarantee we have the most recent rendition of every-thing. This is finished utilizing;

```
sudo apt-get update
```

pursued by;

```
sudo apt-get upgrade
```

With the update done, reboot your pi to impact changes.

Stage 2: Install "dnsmasq" and "hostapd"
Next, we introduce the product that makes it con-ceivable to arrangement the pi as a remote passage and furthermore the product that appoints organize address to gadgets that interface with the AP. We do this by running;

```
sudo apt-get install dnsmasq
```

pursued by;

```
sudo apt-get install hostapd
```

or at the mean time you could consolidate it by running;

```
sudo apt-get install dnsmasq hostapd
```

Stage 3: Stop the product from Running

Since we don't have the product arranged right now there is no point running it, so we handicap them from running in the underground. To do this we run the accompanying directions to stop the systemd activity.

```
sudo systemctl stop dnsmasq

sudo systemctl stop hostapd
```

Stage 4: Configure a Static IP address for the remote Port

Affirm the wlan port on which the remote gadget being utilized is associated. For my Pi, the remote is on wlan0. Setting up the Raspberry Pi to go about as a server expects us to appoint a static IP address to the remote port. This should be possible by altering the dhcpcd config record. To alter the arrangement record, run;

```
sudo nano /etc/dhcpcd.conf
```

Look to the base of the config document and include the accompanying lines.

Interface wlan0

static ip_address=192.168.4.1/24

In the wake of including the lines, the config record should resemble the picture beneath.

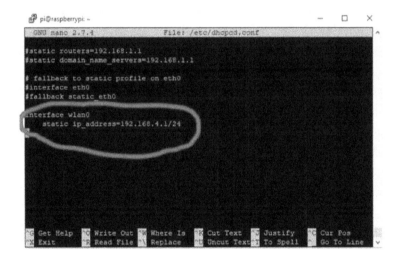

Note: This IP address can be changed to suit your favored arrangement.

Spare the document and leave utilizing; ctrl+x pursued by Y

Restart the dhcpcd administration to impact the progressions made to the setup utilizing;

```
Sudo service dhcpcd restart
```

Stage 5: Configure the dhcpcd server

With a static IP address currently designed for the Raspberry Pi wlan, the following thing is for us to arrange the dhcpcd server as well as give it the scope of IP delivers to be relegated to gadgets that interface with the remote passageway. To do this, we have to alter the arrangement document of the dnsmasq programming however the config record of the product contains an excessive amount of data and a ton could turn out badly If not appropriately altered, so as opposed to altering, we will make another config document with simply the measure of data that is expected to make the remote passage completely useful.

Before making the new config document, we protect the old on by moving and renaming it.

```
sudo mv /etc/dnsmasq.conf /etc/dnsmasq.conf.old
```

At that point dispatch the editorial manager to make another setup document;

sudo nano /etc/dnsmasq.conf

with the editorial manager propelled, duplicate the lines beneath and glue in or type legitimately into it.

Interface = wlan0 #indicate the communication interface which is usually wlan0 for wireless

dhcp-range = 192.168.4.2, 192.168.4.20, 255.255.255.0,24h

the substance of the record should resemble the picture underneath.

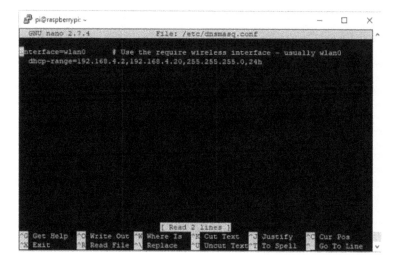

Spare the record and exit. The substance of this config record is simply to indicate the scope of IP address that can be allocated to gadgets associated with the remote passage.

With this done, we will have the option to give a personality to gadgets on our system.
The following arrangement of steps will assist us with designing the passageway have programming, arrangement the ssid, select the encrytpion and so on.

Stage 6: Configure hostapd for SSID and Password

We have to alter the hostapd config file(run sudo nano/and so forth/hostapd/hostapd.conf) to include the different parameters for the remote system being arrangement including the ssid and secret key. Its ought to be noticed that the secret key (passphrase) ought to be somewhere in the range of 8 and 64 characters. Anything lesser won't work.

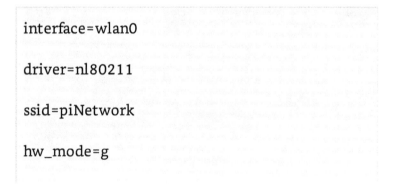

interface=wlan0

driver=nl80211

ssid=piNetwork

hw_mode=g

```
channel=7

wmm_enabled=0

macaddr_acl=0

auth_algs=1

ignore_broadcast_ssid=0

wpa=2

wpa_passphrase=emmanuel # use a very secure
password and not this

wpa_key_mgmt=WPA-PSK

wpa_pairwise=TKIP

rsn_pairwise=CCM
```

The substance of the document should resemble the picture beneath.

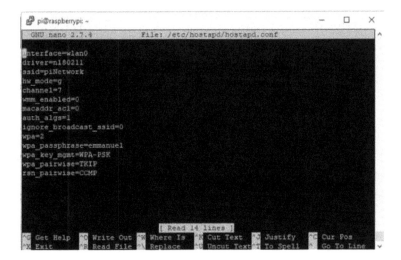

Don't hesitate to change the ssid and secret phrase to suit your needs as well as want.

Spare the config record and exit.

After the config record has been spared, we have to point the hostapd programming to where the config document has been spared. To do this, run;

sudo nano /etc/default/hostapd

discover the line with daemon_conf remarked out as appeared in the picture underneath.

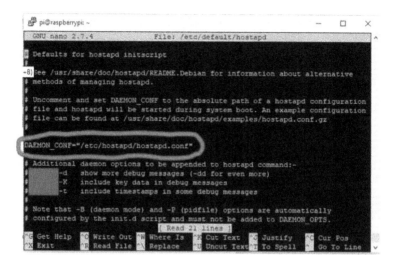

Uncomment the DAEMON_CONF line and include the line underneath in the middle of the statements before the "equivalent to" sign.

/etc/hostapd/hostapd.conf

Stage 7: Fire it up

Since we incapacitated the two programming at first, to permit us design them appropriately, we have to restart the framework after arrangement to impact the changes.

Use;

sudo systemctl start hostapd

41

```
sudo systemctl start dnsmasq
```

Stage 8: Routing and disguise for outbound traffic

We have to include directing and disguise for outbound traffic.

To do this, we have to alter the config document of the systemctl by running:

```
sudo nano /etc/sysctl.conf
```

Uncomment this line net.ipv4.ip_forward=1(highlighted in the picture beneath)

Spare the config record and leave utilizing ctrl+x pursued by y.

Next we move to disguising the outbound traffic. This should be possible by rolling out certain improvements to the iptable principle. To do this, run the accompanying directions:

```
sudo iptables -t nat -A  POSTROUTING -o eth0 -j
MASQUERADE
```

at that point spare the Iptables rule utilizing:

```
sudo sh -c "iptables-save > /etc/iptables.ipv4.nat"
```

Stage 9: Create Wireless Access Point on startup:
For most remote passageway application, it is frequently wanted that the passageway comes up when the framework boots. To actualize this on the raspberry pi, probably the most effortless ways is to add guidelines to run the product in the rc.local document so we put directions to introduce the iptable standards on boot in the rc.local record.

To alter the rc.local document, run:

```
sudo nano /etc/rc.local
```

also, include the accompanying lines at the base of

the framework, just before the leave 0 explanation

```
iptables-restore < /etc/iptables.ipv4.nat
```

Stage 9: Reboot! what's more, Use

At this stage, we have to reboot the framework to impact every one of the progressions and test the remote passage firing up on boot with the iptables rule refreshed.

Reboot the framework utilizing:

```
sudo reboot
```

When the framework returns on, you ought to have the option to get to the remote passage utilizing any Wi-Fi empowered gadget and the secret key utilized during the arrangement.

Accessing the Internet from the Raspberry Pi's Wi-Fi Hotspot

Goodness truly, so I will add a reward instructional exercise to show how the remote passage made can be used to give web association with the gadgets associated with it. The web get to circulated to the gadgets is given through the Ethernet port on the Pi which can be combined with a switch otherwise any comparable gadgets.

To execute this, we have to put a "connect" in the middle of the remote gadget and the Ethernet gadget on the Raspberry Pi (the remote passage) to pass all traffic between the two interfaces. To set this up, we will utilize the extension utils programming. Introduce hostapd and connect utils. While we have introduced hostapd previously, run the establishment again to clear all questions.

```
sudo apt-get install hostapd bridge-utils
```

Next, we stop hostapd in order to arrange the product.

```
sudo systemctl stop hostapd
```

At the point when a scaffold is made, a more significant level build is made over the two ports being spanned and the extension in this manner turns into the system gadget. To avert clashes, we have to stop the designation of IP addresses by the DHCP customer running on the Raspberry Pi to the eth0 and wlan0 ports. This will be finished by altering the config record of the dhcpcd customer to incorporate denyinterfaces wlan0 and denyinterfaces eth0 as appeared in the picture beneath.

The document can be altered by running the direction;

```
sudo nano /etc/dhcpcd.conf
```

Note:

From this point on, guarantee you don't separate the Ethernet link from your PC on the off chance that you are running in headless mode as you will most likely be unable to associate by means of SSH again since we have handicapped the Ethernet port. On the off chance that working with a screen, you don't have anything to fear.

Next, we make another extension called br0

```
sudo brctl addbr br0
```

Next, we interface the ethernet port (eth0) to the scaffold (br0) utilizing;

```
sudo brctl addif br0 eth0
```

Next, we alter the interfaces document utilizing sudo nano/and so forth/arrange/interfaces so different gadgets can work with the extension. Alter the interfaces document to incorporate the data beneath;

```
#Bridge setup

auto br0

iface br0 inet manual

bridge_ports eth0 wlan0
```

Finally we alter the hostapd.conf record to incorporate the scaffold arrangement. This should be possible by running the order: sudo nano/and so forth/hostapd.conf and altering the record to contain the data beneath. Note the scaffold was included underneath the wlan0 interface and the driver line was remarked out.

```
interface=wlan0

bridge=br0

#driver=nl80211

ssid=NameOfNetwork

hw_mode=g

channel=7

wmm_enabled=0

macaddr_acl=0

auth_algs=1

ignore_broadcast_ssid=0

wpa=2

wpa_passphrase=AardvarkBadgerHedgehog

wpa_key_mgmt=WPA-PSK

wpa_pairwise=TKIP
```

```
rsn_pairwise=CCMP
```

With this done, spare the config document and exit.

To impact the progressions made to the Raspberry Pi, reboot the framework. When it returns up, you should now have the option to get to the web by interfacing with the Wireless passageway made by the Raspberry Pi. This obviously will possibly work if web get to

While this undertaking can be utilized to expand Wi-Fi around the house or office or a whole compound, there are a few applications I find exceptionally fascinating and valuable like the raspberry pi as a home mechanization center point so a few Wi-Fi empowered home robotization gadgets can interface with the web utilizing the raspberry pi's remote passage. Do you have some other cool Idea, to which this can be applied, don't hesitate to share by means of the remark area to motivate others.

Testing Raspberry Pi Wireless Access Point:

To test these guidelines, utilize a cell phone or some other gadget equipped for interfacing with a WiFi hotspot organize, you should see the name spring up. You would then be able to associate with it by utilizing that awful secret word we determined "emmanuel". Make certain to utilize a progressively secure secret key when executing. I just utilized that secret phrase to make things simpler to pursue.

Likewise note, it may take some time for the Wireless passage to get obvious after reboot as the Pi needs to boot up before the system exercises start.

That is it for this instructional exercise folks. It's a long one, a debt of gratitude is in order for investing significant energy to peruse. Criticism and remarks are constantly welcome.

Till next time!

3. RASPBERRY PI TWITTER BOT UTILIZING PYTHON

Twitter like most other web based life stages is authoritatively part of our regular day to day existence, either for individual or business use, its become an extraordinary method to associate with the world, either by trolling or sharing significant data. For business particularly, there is constantly an incredible need to plan tweets or robotize things in a single manner or the other. Consider the possibility that there was an approach to do that with almost no human supervision once its everything arrangement, that is the reason for the present instructional exercise, we will concentrate on furnishing our Raspberry Pi with the capacity to post and understand tweets. This turns out to be extremely helpful on account of occasions where you need the Raspberry Pi to take pictures indiscriminately and post them on twitter or when you have to post a string.

The present Tutorial depends vigorously on the python library, Twython, which is a python module for interfacing with twitter. With twython, we could do the vast majority of the things you typically would need to do on your twitter handle like send DMs, Post tweets, read tweets, read DMs, Upload a picture, change DP, Change foundation picture, and significantly more. Twython requires verification from twitter, which can be gotten by making a twitter application. All these will be shrouded in the bit by bit guidelines as we continue.

Gives jump access!

Required Components

The accompanying parts are required to fabricate this task;

- Raspberry pi 2 or 3

- LAN Cable

- Secure Digital Card (8gb Minimum)

- Power source

Discretionary

- Console

- Screen

- Mouse

- HDMI Cable

To continue, we will utilize the Raspbian stretch OS for this instructional exercise and since its arrangement is same as that of the Jessie, I will accept you know about setting up the Raspberry Pi with the Raspbian stretch OS. I likewise need to accept you know how to ssh into the Raspberry Pi utilizing a terminal programming like putty. On the off chance that you have issues with any of the things referenced, there are huge amounts of Raspberry Pi Tutorials on this site can help.

For new Stretch clients (new introduces), you should take note of that SSH is debilitated and you should empower it before you can converse with the raspberry pi over SSH. One approach to do this is to enact it by interfacing a screen and empowering ssh, while the subsequent which is my most loved is by making a document named ssh (with no augmentation) and replicating it to the root organizer on your SD card. This should be possible by embeddings it the SD card into your PC.

With that done, lets arrangement our Raspberry Pi Twitter Bot.

Installing Twython on Raspberry Pi

The main thing we do is introduce the Twython library for the Raspberry Pi which is the thing that we will utilize interface with twitter.

Pursue these means to introduce Twython.

Stage 1: Like we generally do, refresh and overhaul your raspberry pi utilizing the accompanying direction;

```
sudo apt-get update

sudo apt-get upgrade
```

Stage 2: Install python instruments

```
sudo apt-get install python-setuptools
```

Stage 3: introduce pip if not recently introduced.

```
sudo easy_install pip
```

Stage 4: Install twython by means of pip

```
sudo pip install twython
```

After these means, you ought to have Twython introduced and fit to be utilized by python. Next we make the Twitter App.

Create a Twitter App

To have the option to cooperate with twitter from outside the twitter space, we need the twitter API and to approach that, we have to make another twitter application, whose subtleties will at that point be utilized by the Twython library to interface the our python content to twitter.

Pursue the means underneath to get it fully operational.

Stage 1: Sign in to your twitter account and go to this URL https://apps.twitter.com/application/new

Stage 2: Fill in the subtleties. A model is demonstrated as follows.

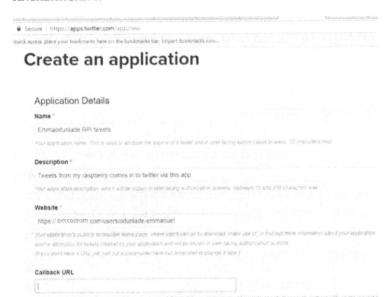

Experience the engineer understanding, on the off chance that you approve of it, hit submit. That is correct, the application is made.

On the following page in the wake of clicking submit, you should see application settings, keys as well as access tokens, as well as authorizations. Experience the consents area and guarantee everything resembles the picture underneath

Details   Settings   Keys and Access Tokens   Permissions

Access

What type of access does your application need?

Read more about our Application Permission Model

○ Read only

● Read and Write

○ Read, Write and Access direct messages

Note:

Changes to the application permission model will only affect access tokens obtained after the permission model change is saved. You will need to re-negotiate existing access tokens to alter the permission level associated with each of your application's users.

Additional Permissions

These additional permissions require that you provide URLs to your application or service's privacy policy and terms of service. You can configure these fields in your Application Settings.

☐ Request email addresses from users

Update Settings

Stage 3: Next we create the entrance tokens which will be utilized to get to twitter from our python content.

Your Access Token

This access token can be used to make API requests on your own account's behalf. Do not share your access token secret with anyone.

Access Token	
Access Token Secret	
Access Level	Read and write
Owner	emmaddundade
Owner ID	

Token Actions

Regenerate My Access Token and Token Secret   Revoke Token Access

Stage 4: You will likewise require the customer mystery and the purchaser key which is additionally found under the keys and access tokens area to set up

the Twython.

With our entrance keys and tokens close by and the Twython library introduced, we are prepared to compose the content with which we will have the option to present messages on or read messages from twitter.

Python Script for Raspberry Pi Twitter Bot:

Guarantee you are in the root organizer by entering the order

```
cd ~
```

In the event that you as of now have an undertaking envelope for your Raspberry Pi ventures, CD into it. if not, it's smarter to make one to keep your work sorted out and across the board place.

So in case you are in the subsequent class how about we make an undertaking organizer utilizing;

```
mkdir rpiprojects
```

PS: you can consider it whatever name you want.

Change catalog to that of the venture envelope:

```
cd rpiprojects
```

at that point open a proofreader to compose your python content;

```
sudo nano pitwits.py
```

You can likewise call this any name you want.

When the proofreader opens, type in the accompanying lines of code,

```
#!/usr/bin/env python

import sys

from twython import Twython
```

```
#enter the keys and secrets inbetween the quotes

consumerKey = ''

consumerSecret = ''

accessKey = ''

accessSecret = ''

api = Twython(consumerKey,consumerSecret,ac-
cessKey,accessSecret)

api.update_status(status=sys.argv)
```

Guarantee to enter the entrance tokens and keys from the twitter application we made before, before sparing and leaving the supervisor. Enter Ctrl + X pursued by Y to spare while leaving the editorial manager.

With the python content all done, we are presently prepared to post a few tweets however before that, we have to make the python content an executable document. We can do this by entering the accompanying in the terminal;

```
sudo chmod +x pitwits.py
```

The content should now be an executable document

and we would now be able to post a tweet by entering the directions as demonstrated as follows;

```
sudo python pitwits.py 'yee-haw, my Pi tweets'
```

Automate the Tweets by Raspberry Pi

So probably the coolest thing we could do is mechanize the information being posted by the PI, so on the off chance that you were chipping away at a temperature and mugginess based undertaking for example and you need the information to be accessible to the overall population, or a traffic tweeting gadget.

All you will require do essentially is incorporate the content that estimates your temperature and moistness for example and make a cron employment to robotize the content.

So in this model I will accept we are at an occasion and I need the raspberry pi to tweet pictures from the occasion self-governingly.

To do this, we will simply roll out a couple of improvements to the pitwits.py and give it another name piimagetwits.py

```
#!/usr/bin/env python

import sys
```

```python
from twython import Twython

import os

import pygame

import pygame.camera

from pygame.locals import *

#enter the keys and secrets inbetween the quotes

consumerKey = ''

consumerSecret = "

accessKey = ''

accessSecret = ''

pygame.init()

pygame.camera.init()

api = Twython(consumerKey,consumerSecret,accessKey,accessSecret)

cam = pygame.camera.Camera("/dev/video0", (640,480))
```

```
cam.start()

image = cam.get_image()

pygame.image.save(image,'eventimg.jpg')

photo = open('webcam.jpg','rb')

api.update_status_with_media(media=photo, sta-
tus='Event photo Updates ')
```

Spare and exit.

At that point as we did the main content, make this an executable as well.

```
Sudo chmod +x piimagetwits.py
```

At that point continue to making a cron work with it. Run the order:

```
sudo crontab -e
```

To make a cron employment and include these lines beneath it relying upon the planning you need.

*/60 * python/home/pi/rpiprojects/piimagetwits.py

This cron work runs each moment because of the

planning demonstrated by the bullets, yet you can set your own planning as depicted beneath.

```
# Edit this file to introduce tasks to be run by cron.
#
# Each task to run has to be defined through a single line
# indicating with different fields when the task will be run
# and what command to run for the task
#
# To define the time you can provide concrete values for
# minute (m), hour (h), day of month (dom), month (mon),
# and day of week (dow) or use '*' in these fields (for 'any').#
# Notice that tasks will be started based on the cron's system
# daemon's notion of time and timezones.
#
# Output of the crontab jobs (including errors) is sent through
# email to the user the crontab file belongs to (unless redirected).
#
# For example, you can run a backup of all your user accounts
# at 5 a.m every week with:
# 0 5 * * 1 tar -zcf /var/backups/home.tgz /home/
```

More data on the best way to utilize the cron work timing can be found in the depiction of any of the manager you decided to utilize. For instance I lean toward vim for no specific explanation and here is a portrayal of how to utilize the planning.

Raspberry Pi Twitter Bot in Action:

So I posted several tweets, brought about the ideal result.

```
pi@raspberrypi:                              mine, they are t
pi@raspberrypi:                              e, the machine i
                                             T merges with #A
I. #TweetsFromMy
pi@raspberrypi:                              with a #Raspberry
pi could very mu                             #Neuralink, ok,n
ew spare time ha
pi@raspberrypi:
```

That is it for this instructional exercise folks, don't hesitate to drop any question you may have in the remark area, and furthermore tail me on twitter: @emmaodunlade to see increasingly magnificent tweets from my mi pi.

Till next time.

4. REMOTE CONTROLLED CAR USING RASPBERRY PI AND BLUETOOTH

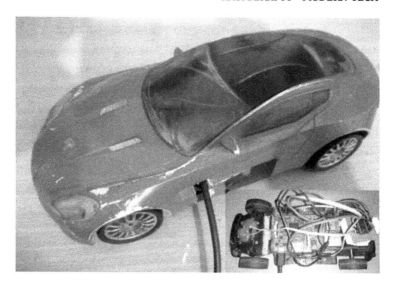

Raspberry Pi is extremely prominent for IoT ventures in light of its consistent capacity of remote correspondence over the web. Raspberry Pi 3 has inbuilt Wi-Fi and Bluetooth, and Bluetooth is an extremely well known remote correspondence Protocol. Today we going to fabricate a Remote Controlled Car utilizing Raspberry Pi 3 and Bluetooth, here we will utilize Smart Phone as a remote to control the vehicle. We have recently constructed made this RC vehicle utilizing Arduino.

Here we are utilizing Raspberry Pi 3 which have inbuilt Bluetooth, so we don't have to utilize any outside USB Bluetooth dongle. Here we are utilizing RF-COMM Bluetooth convention for remote correspondence.

Programming for Bluetooth in Python pursues the

attachment programming model and interchanges between the Bluetooth gadgets is done through RF-COMM attachment. RFCOMM (Radio Frequency Communication) is a Bluetooth Protocol which gave copied RS-232 sequential ports and furthermore called as Serial Port Emulation. Bluetooth sequential port profile depends on this convention. RFCOMM is mainstream in Bluetooth applications due to its wide help and publically accessible API. It is bound to L2CAP convention.

In case you have Raspberry Pi 2, at that point you either need to utilize outer Bluetooth dongle or Bluetooth module HC-06. Check our past activities for utilizing these outside Bluetooth gadgets: Controlling Raspberry Pi GPIO utilizing Android App over Bluetooth and Raspberry Pi controlled Home Appliances.

Installing Required Packages for Bluetooth Communication:

Prior to beginning, we have to introduce some product for setting up Bluetooth correspondence in Raspberry Pi. You ought to have a Raspbian Jessie introduced memory card prepared with Raspberry Pi. Check this article to introduce the Raspbian OS and beginning with Raspberry Pi. So now we first need to refresh the Raspbian utilizing beneath directions:

```
sudo apt-get update
```

```
sudo apt-get upgrade
```

At that point we have to introduce not many Bluetooth related bundles:

```
sudo apt-get install bluetooth blueman bluez
```

At that point reboot the Raspberry Pi:

```
sudo reboot
```

BlueZ is an open source undertaking and authority Linux Bluetooth convention stack. It underpins all the center Bluetooth conventions and now become piece of legitimate Linux Kernel.

Blueman gives the Desktop interface to oversee and control the Bluetooth gadgets.

At last we need python Library for Bluetooth correspondence with the goal that we can send and get information through RFCOMM utilizing Python language:

```
sudo apt-get install python-bluetooth
```

Likewise introduce the GPIO bolster libraries for

Raspberry Pi:

```
sudo apt-get install python-rpi.gpio
```

Presently we are finished with introducing required bundles for Bluetooth correspondence in Raspberry Pi.

Pairing Devices with Raspberry Pi over Bluetooth:

Matching Bluetooth Devices, similar to cell phone, with Raspberry Pi is extremely simple. Here we have matched our Android Smart telephone with Raspberry Pi. We have recently introduced BlueZ in Pi, which gives an order line utility called "bluetoothctl" to deal with our Bluetooth gadgets.

Presently open the bluetoothctl utility by underneath order:

```
sudo bluetoothctl
```

You can check every one of the directions of bluetoothctl utility by composing 'help'. For the present we have to enter underneath directions in given request:

```
[bluetooth]# power on
```

```
[bluetooth]# agent on

[bluetooth]# discoverable on

[bluetooth]# pairable on

[bluetooth]# scan on
```

After the keep going order "filter on", you will see your Bluetooth gadget (Mobile telephone) in the rundown. Ensure that your portable has Bluetooth turned on and noticeable by close by gadgets. At that point duplicate the MAC address of you gadget and pair it by utilizing given direction:

```
pair <address of your phone>
```

At that point you will be provoked for Passcode or Pin in your Terminal reassure then type password there and press enter. At that point type the equivalent password in your cell phone when incited and you are currently effectively combined with Raspberry Pi. Here is the direct YouTube connect.

As told before, you can likewise utilize Desktop interface to combine the Mobile telephone. In the wake of introducing Blueman, you will see a Bluetooth symbol in right half of your Raspberry Pi work area as demonstrated as follows, utilizing which you can without much of a stretch do the matching.

Selecting the Toy Car:

In this Raspberry Pi Controlled Car venture we have utilized a toy vehicle for exhibit. Here we have chosen a RF toy vehicle with moving left-right controlling element. In the wake of purchasing this vehicle we have supplanted its RF circuit with our Raspberry circuit. This vehicle has two DC engines, one to pivot two front haggle one is to turn two back wheels. Front side engine is utilized for provide guidance to vehicle implies turning left or right side (like genuine vehicle directing component). What's more, back side engine is utilized for driving the vehicle in forward and in reverse heading. A Bluetooth of Raspberry is utilized to get order remotely from android telephone to control the vehicle.

You can utilize any toy vehicle which has two DC Motors to turn front and Rear Wheels.

Circuit Diagram and Explanation:

In this Remote Controlled Car, we just need to interface Raspberry Pi with 2 engines utilizing L293D module. For fueling the Raspberry Pi and vehicle we have utilized a portable power bank. The portable power bank is sufficient to control the Raspberry Pi and's engines yet when we put control bank over vehicle then because of the overwhelming load of versatile power bank vehicle would not have the option to move appropriately. So we prescribe to utilize the low weight control supply or Lithium batteries for fueling the framework. Every combination is appeared in circuit outline underneath. Additionally, check our Robotics segment to become familiar with controlling Motors with various advancements.

Note: don't put more than 5v to the raspberry pi.

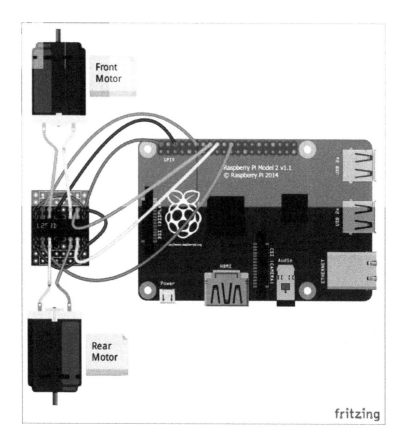

This circuit has been made on Perf Board for this undertaking, so that there is less weight on the vehicle.

Controlling Car Remotely with Android App Blue-Term:

Presently in the wake of setting up every one of the things and effectively take a stab at paring the Smart Phone over bluetooth, we have to introduce an An-

droid App for speaking with Raspberry Pi utilizing a Bluetooth Serial Adapter, so we can manage the GPIO pins of Raspberry Pi. As told before RFCOMM/SPP convention imitates sequential correspondence over Bluetooth, so we introduced here BlueTerm App which bolsters this convention.

Terminal emulator to connect to any serial device with bluetooth serial adapter.

You can likewise utilize some other Bluetooth Terminal App which bolsters correspondence by means of RFCOMM attachment.

Presently in the wake of downloading and introducing the BlueTerm App, run the beneath given Python Program from the terminal and associate the matched raspberrypi gadget from the BlueTerm App simultaneously.

After fruitful association you will see connected:raspberrypi at the upper right corner of the App as demonstrated as follows:

Presently you can simply enter the accompanying directions from the BlueTerm application to make the vehicle moving in the ideal heading. Press 'q' to leave the program. You can utilize Google Voice Typing Keyboard to manage this vehicle utilizing your Voice.

Directions:

F - Forward Move

B - Backward Move

S - Stop

L - Forward Left Move

R - Forward Right Move

A - Backward Left Move

P - Backward Right Move

Q - Quit

Python Programming:

Python Program for Controlling Raspberry Pi GPIO with Android App is basic and plain as day. Just we have to get familiar with a tad about the code identified with Bluetooth RFCOMM correspondence. Generally, its equivalent like controlling any robot or vehicle by making engine's stick high or low. The total program is given beneath in the Code segment.

Initially, we have to import the Bluetooth attachment library which empowers us to control Bluetooth with Python language; we have introduced the library for the equivalent in the past area.

```
import Bluetooth
```

At that point we incorporated some more header documents and characterize pins for engines put them default low.

```
import bluetooth

import time

import RPi.GPIO as GPIO

m11=18

m12=23
```

```
m21=24

m22=25

GPIO.setwarnings(False)

GPIO.setmode(GPIO.BCM)

GPIO.setup(m11, GPIO.OUT)

GPIO.setup(m12, GPIO.OUT)

GPIO.setup(m21, GPIO.OUT)

GPIO.setup(m22, GPIO.OUT)

GPIO.output(m11, 0)

GPIO.output(m12, 0)

GPIO.output(m21, 0)

GPIO.output(m22, 0)
```

The following is the code liable for Bluetooth correspondence:

```
server_socket=bluetooth.Bluetooth-
Socket(bluetooth.RFCOMM)
```

```
port = 1

server_socket.bind(("",port))

server_socket.listen(1)

client_socket,address = server_socket.accept()

print "Accepted connection from ",address
```

Here we can comprehend them line by line:

server_socket=bluetooth.Bluetooth-Socket(bluetooth.RFCOMM): Creating attachment for Bluetooth RFCOMM correspondence.

server_socket.bind(("", port):- Server ties the content on have " to port.

server_socket.listen(1): Server tunes in to acknowledge each association in turn.

client_socket, address = server_socket.accept(): Server acknowledges customer's association ask for and appoint the macintosh address to the variable location, client_socket is the customer's attachment

After this we have made a few capacities that are liable for moving vehicle in the ideal heading: def left_side_forward(), def right_side_forward(), def forward(), def left_side_reverse(), def right_side_reverse(), def reverse()def stop(). These capacities will be called individually when we press L, R, F, A, P, B, S from the Mobile blueTerm application and the vehicle will move likewise.

```
data=""

while 1:

    data= client_socket.recv(1024)

    print "Received: %s" % data

    if(data == "F"):

      forward()

    elif(data == "L"):

      left_side_forward()

    elif(data == "R"):

      right_side_forward()

    elif(data == "B"):

      reverse()

    elif(data == "A"):
```

```
    left_side_reverse()

  elif(data == "P"):

    right_side_reverse()

  elif data == "S":

    stop()

  elif(data == "Q"):

    print ("Quit")

    break

client_socket.close()

server_socket.close()
```

information = client_socket.recv(1024): Receive information through the customer attachment client_socket and dole out it to the variable information. Most extreme 1024 characters can be gotten at once.

At last, after all the programming, close the customer and server association utilizing underneath code:

```
client_socket.close()
```

```
server_socket.close()
```

Code

```
import bluetooth
import time
import RPi.GPIO as GPIO
m11 = 18
m12 = 23
m21 = 24
m22 = 25
GPIO.setwarnings(False)
GPIO.setmode(GPIO.BCM)
GPIO.setup(m11, GPIO.OUT)
GPIO.setup(m12, GPIO.OUT)
GPIO.setup(m21, GPIO.OUT)
GPIO.setup(m22, GPIO.OUT)
GPIO.output(m11 , 0)
GPIO.output(m12 , 0)
GPIO.output(m21, 0)
GPIO.output(m22, 0)
server_socket=bluetooth.Bluetooth-
Socket( bluetooth.RFCOMM )
port = 1
server_socket.bind(("",port))
server_socket.listen(1)


client_socket,address = server_socket.accept()
print "Accepted connection from ",address
```

```
def left_side_forward():
  print "FORWARD LEFT"
  GPIO.output(m21 , 1)
  GPIO.output(m22 , 0)
  time.sleep(.5)
  GPIO.output(m11 , 1)
  GPIO.output(m12 , 0)
def right_side_forward():
  print "FORWARD RIGHT"
  GPIO.output(m21 , 1)
  GPIO.output(m22 , 0)
  time.sleep(.5)
  GPIO.output(m11 , 0)
  GPIO.output(m12 , 1)
def forward():
  print "FORWARD"
  GPIO.output(m11 , 0)
  GPIO.output(m12 , 0)
  GPIO.output(m21 , 1)
  GPIO.output(m22 , 0)
def left_side_reverse():
  print "BACKWARD LEFT"
  GPIO.output(m21 , 0)
  GPIO.output(m22 , 1)
  time.sleep(.5)
  GPIO.output(m11 , 1)
  GPIO.output(m12 , 0)
def right_side_reverse():
  print "BACKWARD RIGHT"
  GPIO.output(m21 , 0)
```

```
 GPIO.output(m22 , 1)
 time.sleep(.5)
 GPIO.output(m11 , 0)
 GPIO.output(m12 , 1)
def reverse():
 print "BACKWARD"
 GPIO.output(m11 , 0)
 GPIO.output(m12 , 0)
 GPIO.output(m21 , 0)
 GPIO.output(m22 , 1)
def stop():
 print "STOP"
 GPIO.output(m11 , 0)
 GPIO.output(m12 , 0)
 GPIO.output(m21 , 0)
 GPIO.output(m22 , 0)


data=""
while 1:
    data= client_socket.recv(1024)
    print "Received: %s" % data
    if(data == "F"):
      forward()
    elif(data == "L"):
      left_side_forward()
    elif(data == "R"):
      right_side_forward()
    elif(data == "B"):
      reverse()
    elif(data == "A"):
```

```
    left_side_reverse()
  elif(data == "P"):
    right_side_reverse()
  elif data == "S":
    stop()
  elif(data == "Q"):
    print ("Quit")
    break
client_socket.close()
server_socket.close()
```

❖ ❖ ❖

5. UNIQUE MARK SENSOR INTERFACING WITH RASPBERRY PI

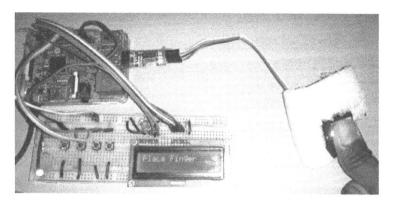

Unique mark Sensor, which we used to see in Sci-Fi moives not many years back, is currently gotten regular to confirm the character of an individual for different purposes. In present time we can see unique mark based frameworks wherever in our day by day life like for participation in workplaces, representative confirmation in banks, for money withdrawal or stores in ATMs, for character check in government workplaces and so on. We have as of now interfaced it with Arduino, today we are gonna to interface Finger-Print Sensor with Raspberry Pi. Utilizing this Raspberry Pi FingerPrint System, we can enlist new fingerprints in the framework and can erase the as of now sustained fingerprints.

Required Components:

- Raspberry Pi
- Fingerprint Module
- USB to Serial converter
- 16x2 LCD

- Push buttons
- Bread Board or PCB (ordered from JLCPCB)
- 10k pot
- Jumper wires
- Resistor 150 ohm -1 k ohm (optional)
- LED (optional)

Circuit Diagram and Explanation:

In this Raspberry Pi Finger Print sensor interfacing venture, we have utilized a 4 push catches: 1 for enlisting the new finger pring, one for erasing the as of now encouraged fingerprints and rest two for increase/decrement the situation of as of now bolstered Finger prints. A LED is utilized for sign that unique mark sensor is prepared to take finger for coordinating. Here we have utilized a unique mark module which deals with UART. So here we have interfaced this unique mark module with Raspberry Pi utilizing a USB to Serial converter.

Along these lines, above all else, we have to make the all the necessary association as appeared in Circuit Diagram underneath. Associations are basic, we have quite recently associated unique mark module to Raspberry Pi USB port by utilizing USB to Serial converter. A 16x2 LCD is utilized for showing all messages. A 10k pot is additionally utilized with LCD for controlling the differentiation of the equivalent. 16x2 LCD pins RS, EN, d4, d5, d6, and d7 are associated with GPIO Pin 18, 23, 24, 25, 8 and 7 of Raspberry Pi individually. Four push catches are associated with GPIO Pin 5, 6, 13 and 19 of Raspberry Pi. Driven is likewise associated at stick 26 of RPI.

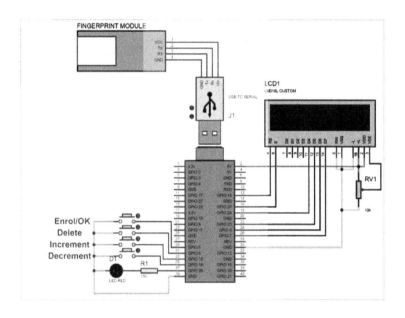

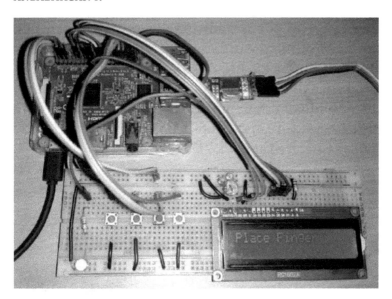

Installing Library for Finger Print Sensor:

In the wake of making every one of the associations we have to control up Raspberry Pi and prepare it with terminal open. Presently we have to introduce unique mark library for Raspberry Pi in python language by following the beneath steps.

Stage 1: To introduce this library, root benefits are required. So first we enter in root by given direction:

```
sudo bash
```

Stage 2: Then download some necessary bundles by utilizing given directions:

wget   –O   –   http://apt.pm-codeworks.de/pm-codeworks.de.gpg | apt-key add –

wget   http://apt.pm-codeworks.de/pm-codeworks.list -P /etc/apt/sources.list.d/

Stage 3: After this, we have to refresh the Raspberry pi and introduce the downloaded unique mark sensor library:

sudo apt-get update

> sudo apt-get install python-fingerprint –yes

```
root@raspberrypi:/home/pi# apt-get install python-fingerprint --yes
Reading package lists... Done
Building dependency tree
Reading state information... Done
python-fingerprint is already the newest version.
The following packages were automatically installed and are no longer required:
  libasn1-8-heimdal libgssapi3-heimdal libhcrypto4-heimdal
  libheimbase1-heimdal libheimntlm0-heimdal libhx509-5-heimdal
  libkrb5-26-heimdal libroken18-heimdal libwind0-heimdal
Use 'apt-get autoremove' to remove them.
0 upgraded, 0 newly installed, 0 to remove and 294 not upgraded.
root@raspberrypi:/home/pi# exit
exit
pi@raspberrypi:~ $
```

Stage 4: After introducing library now we have to check USB port on which your unique mark sensor is associated, by utilizing given the order:

> ls /dev/ttyUSB*

Presently supplant the USB port no., with the USB port you got over the screen and supplant it in the python code. Complete Python code is given toward the finish of this undertaking.

Operation of Fingerprint Sensor with Raspberry Pi:

Activity of this venture is basic, simply run the python code and there will be few introduction messages over LCD and afterward client will be approached to Place Finger on Finger Print Sensor. Presently by putting a finger over unique mark module, we can check whether our fingerprints are as of now put away or not. In the event that your unique finger impression is put away, at that point LCD will show the message with the putting away position of unique mark like 'Wellspring at Pos:2' else it will show 'No Match Found'.

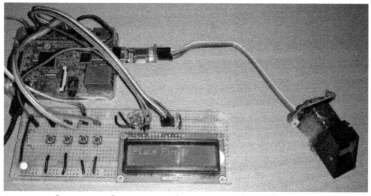

Presently to select a unique mark, client needs to press enlist fasten and adhere to the guidelines messages on LCD screen.

In the event that the client needs to erase any of fingerprints, at that point the client needs to press erase button. After which, LCD will request the situation of the unique finger impression which is to be erased. Presently by utilizing another two push button for augmentation and decrement, client can choose the situation of spared Finger Print and press enlist button (right now select catch carry on as Ok button) to erase that unique mark.

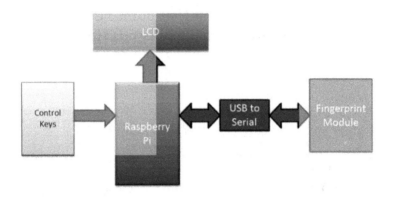

Python Programming:

Python for interfacing Finger Print Sensor with RPi is simple with utilizing unique mark library capacities. Yet, in case the client needs to interface it himself, at that point it will be tad hard just because. In unique mark sensor datasheets, everything is given that is required for interfacing a similar module. A GitHub code is accessible to test your Raspberry pi with Finger Print sensor.

Here we have utilized the library so we simply need to call library work. In code, first we have to import libraries like unique mark, GPIO and time, at that point we have to characterize pins for LCD, LED and push catches.

```
import time

from pyfingerprint.pyfingerprint import PyFinger-
```

```
print

import RPi.GPIO as gpio

RS =18

EN =23

D4 =24

D5 =25

D6 =8

D7 =7

enrol=5

delet=6

inc=13

dec=19

led=26

HIGH=1

LOW=0
```

After this, we have to introduce and provide guidance to the chose pins

```
gpio.setwarnings(False)

gpio.setmode(gpio.BCM)

gpio.setup(RS, gpio.OUT)

gpio.setup(EN, gpio.OUT)

gpio.setup(D4, gpio.OUT)

gpio.setup(D5, gpio.OUT)

gpio.setup(D6, gpio.OUT)

gpio.setup(D7, gpio.OUT)

gpio.setup(enrol,   gpio.IN,   pull_up_down=gpio.
PUD_UP)

gpio.setup(delet,   gpio.IN,   pull_up_down=gpio.
PUD_UP)

gpio.setup(inc,   gpio.IN,   pull_up_down=gpio.
PUD_UP)
```

```
gpio.setup(dec,    gpio.IN,    pull_up_down=gpio.
PUD_UP)

gpio.setup(led, gpio.OUT)
```

Presently we have instated unique mark Sensor

```
try:

        f  =  PyFingerprint('/dev/ttyUSB0',  57600,
0xFFFFFFFF, 0x00000000)

  if ( f.verifyPassword() = = False ):

        raise ValueError('The given fingerprint sensor
password is wrong!')

  except Exception as e:

  print('Exception message: ' + str(e))

  exit(1)
```

We have thought of some capacity to instate and
drive the LCD, check the total code underneath in
code area:

```
def begin(), def lcdcmd(ch), def lcdwrite(ch), def lcd-
```

```
print(Str), def setCursor(x,y)
```

Subsequent to composing all LCD driver capacities, we have set capacities for unique finger impression selecting, looking and erasing.

def enrollFinger() work is utilized for select or spare the new fingerprints.

def searchFinger() work is utilized to searthc the as of now put away fingerprints

def deleteFinger() functinos is utilized to deoted the effectively spared unique mark by squeezing the correspontind push button.

All over capacity's Code is given the in python code given underneath.

After this, at last, we have to instate framework by in while 1 circle by requesting to Place Finger on unique mark sensor and afterward framework will check whether this finger impression it substantial or not and show the outcomes as needs be.

```
begin()

lcdcmd(0x01)

lcdprint("FingerPrint ")
```

```
lcdcmd(0xc0)

lcdprint("Interfacing")

time.sleep(3)

lcdcmd(0x01)

lcdprint("Hello world")

lcdcmd(0xc0)

lcdprint("Welcomes You ")

time.sleep(3)

flag=0

lcdclear()

while 1:

  gpio.output(led, HIGH)

  lcdcmd(1)

  lcdprint("Place Finger")

  if gpio.input(enrol) == 0:
```

```
    gpio.output(led, LOW)

    enrollFinger()

  elif gpio.input(delet) == 0:

    gpio.output(led, LOW)

    while gpio.input(delet) == 0:

      time.sleep(0.1)

    deleteFinger()

  else:

    searchFinger()
```

Complete Python Code is given beneath.

Code

```
import time
from pyfingerprint.pyfingerprint import PyFinger-
print
import RPi.GPIO as gpio
RS = 18
EN = 23
D4 = 24
```

```
D5 =25
D6 =8
D7 =7
enrol=5
delet=6
inc=13
dec=19
led=26
HIGH=1
LOW=0
gpio.setwarnings(False)
gpio.setmode(gpio.BCM)
gpio.setup(RS, gpio.OUT)
gpio.setup(EN, gpio.OUT)
gpio.setup(D4, gpio.OUT)
gpio.setup(D5, gpio.OUT)
gpio.setup(D6, gpio.OUT)
gpio.setup(D7, gpio.OUT)
gpio.setup(enrol,    gpio.IN,    pull_up_down=gpio.
PUD_UP)
gpio.setup(delet,    gpio.IN,    pull_up_down=gpio.
PUD_UP)
gpio.setup(inc,    gpio.IN,    pull_up_down=gpio.
PUD_UP)
gpio.setup(dec,    gpio.IN,    pull_up_down=gpio.
PUD_UP)
gpio.setup(led, gpio.OUT)
try:
        f = PyFingerprint('/dev/ttyUSB0', 57600,
0xFFFFFFFF, 0x00000000)
```

```python
  if ( f.verifyPassword() == False ):
    raise ValueError('The given fingerprint sensor pass-
word is wrong!')
except Exception as e:
  print('Exception message: ' + str(e))
  exit(1)
def begin():
 lcdcmd(0x33)
 lcdcmd(0x32)
 lcdcmd(0x06)
 lcdcmd(0x0C)
 lcdcmd(0x28)
 lcdcmd(0x01)
 time.sleep(0.0005)


def lcdcmd(ch):
 gpio.output(RS, 0)
 gpio.output(D4, 0)
 gpio.output(D5, 0)
 gpio.output(D6, 0)
 gpio.output(D7, 0)
 if ch&0x10==0x10:
  gpio.output(D4, 1)
 if ch&0x20==0x20:
  gpio.output(D5, 1)
 if ch&0x40==0x40:
  gpio.output(D6, 1)
 if ch&0x80==0x80:
  gpio.output(D7, 1)
 gpio.output(EN, 1)
```

```
time.sleep(0.005)
gpio.output(EN, 0)
# Low bits
gpio.output(D4, 0)
gpio.output(D5, 0)
gpio.output(D6, 0)
gpio.output(D7, 0)
if ch&0x01 ==0x01:
 gpio.output(D4, 1)
if ch&0x02 ==0x02:
 gpio.output(D5, 1)
if ch&0x04 ==0x04:
 gpio.output(D6, 1)
if ch&0x08 ==0x08:
 gpio.output(D7, 1)
gpio.output(EN, 1)
time.sleep(0.005)
gpio.output(EN, 0)


def lcdwrite(ch):
 gpio.output(RS, 1)
 gpio.output(D4, 0)
 gpio.output(D5, 0)
 gpio.output(D6, 0)
 gpio.output(D7, 0)
 if ch&0x10==0x10:
  gpio.output(D4, 1)
 if ch&0x20==0x20:
  gpio.output(D5, 1)
 if ch&0x40==0x40:
```

```
 gpio.output(D6, 1)
 if ch&0x80==0x80:
  gpio.output(D7, 1)
 gpio.output(EN, 1)
 time.sleep(0.005)
 gpio.output(EN, 0)
 # Low bits
 gpio.output(D4, 0)
 gpio.output(D5, 0)
 gpio.output(D6, 0)
 gpio.output(D7, 0)
 if ch&0x01==0x01:
  gpio.output(D4, 1)
 if ch&0x02==0x02:
  gpio.output(D5, 1)
 if ch&0x04==0x04:
  gpio.output(D6, 1)
 if ch&0x08==0x08:
  gpio.output(D7, 1)
 gpio.output(EN, 1)
 time.sleep(0.005)
 gpio.output(EN, 0)
def lcdclear():
 lcdcmd(0x01)


def lcdprint(Str):
 l=0;
 l=len(Str)
 for i in range(l):
  lcdwrite(ord(Str[i]))
```

```
def setCursor(x,y):
  if y == 0:
    n=128+x
  elif y == 1:
    n=192+x
  lcdcmd(n)
def enrollFinger():
  lcdcmd(1)
  lcdprint("Enrolling Finger")
  time.sleep(2)
  print('Waiting for finger...')
  lcdcmd(1)
  lcdprint("Place Finger")
  while ( f.readImage() == False ):
    pass
  f.convertImage(0x01)
  result = f.searchTemplate()
  positionNumber = result[0]
  if( positionNumber >= 0 ):
    print('Template already exists at position #' + str(
positionNumber))
    lcdcmd(1)
    lcdprint("Finger ALready")
    lcdcmd(192)
    lcdprint(" Exists  ")
    time.sleep(2)
    return
  print('Remove finger...')
  lcdcmd(1)
```

```
  lcdprint("Remove Finger")
  time.sleep(2)
  print('Waiting for same finger again...')
  lcdcmd(1)
  lcdprint("Place Finger")
  lcdcmd(192)
  lcdprint("  Again  ")
  while ( f.readImage() == False ):
    pass
  f.convertImage(0x02)
  if ( f.compareCharacteristics() == 0 ):
    print "Fingers do not match"
    lcdcmd(1)
    lcdprint("Finger Did not")
    lcdcmd(192)
    lcdprint("  Mactched  ")
    time.sleep(2)
    return
  f.createTemplate()
  positionNumber = f.storeTemplate()
  print('Finger enrolled successfully!')
  lcdcmd(1)
  lcdprint("Stored at Pos:")
  lcdprint(str(positionNumber))
  lcdcmd(192)
  lcdprint("successfully")
  print('New template position #' + str(positionNum-
ber))
  time.sleep(2)
def searchFinger():
```

```
    try:
      print('Waiting for finger...')
      while( f.readImage() == False ):
        #pass
        time.sleep(.5)
        return
      f.convertImage(0x01)
      result = f.searchTemplate()
      positionNumber = result[0]
      accuracyScore = result[1]
      if positionNumber == -1 :
        print('No match found!')
        lcdcmd(1)
        lcdprint("No Match Found")
        time.sleep(2)
        return
      else:
          print('Found template at position #' + str(posi-
tionNumber))
        lcdcmd(1)
        lcdprint("Found at Pos:")
        lcdprint(str(positionNumber))
        time.sleep(2)
    except Exception as e:
      print('Operation failed!')
      print('Exception message: ' + str(e))
      exit(1)


def deleteFinger():
  positionNumber = 0
```

```
 count=0
 lcdcmd(1)
 lcdprint("Delete Finger")
 lcdcmd(192)
 lcdprint("Position: ")
 lcdcmd(0xca)
 lcdprint(str(count))
  while gpio.input(enrol) == True:   # here enrol key
means ok
   if gpio.input(inc) == False:
    count=count+1
    if count>1000:
     count=1000
    lcdcmd(0xca)
    lcdprint(str(count))
    time.sleep(0.2)
   elif gpio.input(dec) == False:
    count=count-1
    if count<0:
     count=0
    lcdcmd(0xca)
    lcdprint(str(count))
    time.sleep(0.2)
 positionNumber=count
 if f.deleteTemplate(positionNumber) == True :
   print('Template deleted!')
   lcdcmd(1)
   lcdprint("Finger Deleted");
   time.sleep(2)
begin()
```

```
lcdcmd(0x01)
lcdprint("FingerPrint ")
lcdcmd(0xc0)
lcdprint("Interfacing")
time.sleep(3)
lcdcmd(0x01)
lcdprint("Hello world")
lcdcmd(0xc0)
lcdprint("Welcomes You ")
time.sleep(3)
flag=0
lcdclear()
while 1:
  gpio.output(led, HIGH)
  lcdcmd(1)
  lcdprint("Place Finger")
  if gpio.input(enrol) == 0:
    gpio.output(led, LOW)
    enrollFinger()
  elif gpio.input(delet) == 0:
    gpio.output(led, LOW)
    while gpio.input(delet) == 0:
      time.sleep(0.1)
    deleteFinger()
  else:
    searchFinger()
```

❖ ❖ ❖

6. RASPBERRY PI PRINT SERVER: SETUP A NETWORK SERVER UTILIZING CUPS

Raspberry Pi Print Server using CUPS

To make your printer available from different gadgets or PCs, possibly you need a Wi-Fi printer or need an expensive arrangement to construct a Network Printer. So in this period of celebrations, what might be an ideal blessing than a Network Printer (did I simply give somebody an Idea?) yet as opposed to burning through several dollars for this new procurement, imagine a scenario in which you could do likewise by including a $35 Raspberry Pi 3 to that old printer laying around your work area. Indeed I thought it'd be magnificent as well!

Introduction to Print Server and CUPS:

Print Server can interface different PCs to a solitary or various printers wired or remotely. With the assistance of the Print server, you can get to your printer with different gadgets and can send the print order from any of the associated gadgets to the printer to print any archive.

For this Raspberry Pi Print Server instructional exercise, we will make a Network Printer with the guide of the Raspberry Pi 3 and the god-like CUPS which makes everything conceivable.

CUPS (Common Unix Printing System) is a printing framework for UNIX like working frameworks based PCs. It gives PCs on which it is running the capacity to go about as a print server. A PC running CUPS can acknowledge employments from customer gadgets, process them and give it to the fitting printer to print.

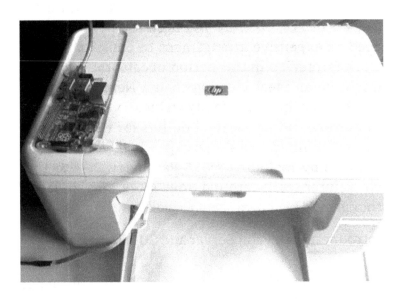

All most all printers are upheld by CUPS particularly

HP printers since HP works its own open source venture. Other printer models that are not legitimately bolstered by CUPS may have nonexclusive drivers that are good which gives fundamental printing capacities. A rundown of printers bolstered by CUPS can be found at this appended connections.

Required Components

Here, we will require the accompanying parts, some of which you may unquestionably have laying around and won't have to purchase.

- Raspberry Pi 3
- USB printer
- Secure Digital Card (8Giga Byte at least)
- Power Supply for the Pi
- Ethernet Cable

To continue, we will utilize the Raspbian stretch OS for this instructional exercise and since its arrangement is same as that of the Jessie, I will expect you know about setting up the Raspberry Pi with the Raspbian stretch OS. I likewise need to expect you know how to ssh into the Raspberry Pi utilizing a terminal programming like putty. In case you have issues with any of the things referenced, there are huge amounts of Raspberry Pi Tutorials on this site can help.

With your Pi primed and ready, Let's make a Raspberry Pi Print Server!

Setting up Network Printer on Raspberry Pi:

This area will bring us through a progression of steps that will finish in the establishment of CUPS on your Raspberry Pi.
Stage 1: Upgrade the Pi

Sort of a custom, first thing for the entirety of my activities is refreshing the Raspberry Pi, by doing this you guarantee your pi has all the most recent updates to the OS you are working with.

To do this we use;

```
sudo apt-get update

sudo apt-get upgrade
```

With this done, reboot the pi utilizing;

```
sudo reboot
```

Sit tight for the reboot procedure and login once more

Stage 2: Install Print Server Software CUPS

With the update done the following line of activity is to introduce our print server programming CUPS.

To do this run;

```
sudo apt-get install cups
```

This will take some time yet will introduce CUPS and different conditions like Samba, perl and a few other programming or libraries.

Stage 3: Configure CUPS

With Installation done, its opportunity to look at the design document of CUPS. A few settings that for the most part influence how cups functions, similar to the port on which cups convey which is as a matter of course 631, port can be changed here.

The config record can be gotten to utilizing;

```
sudo nano /etc/cups/cupsd.conf
```

Change/add the accompanying lines to the arrangement document.

```
# Only listen for connections from the local machine.

#Listen localhost:631
```

#CHANGED TO LISTEN TO LOCAL LAN

Port 631

Restrict access to the server...

<Location />

  Order allow,deny

  Allow @Local

</Location>

Restrict access to the admin pages...

<Location /admin>

  Order allow,deny

  Allow @Local

</Location>

Restrict access to configuration files...

<Location /admin/conf>

  AuthType Default

Require user @SYSTEM

Order allow,deny

Allow @Local

</Location>

Spare the document utilizing ctrl+X pursued by y and afterward enter.

In the wake of sparing, restart CUPS to impact the progressions to the arrangement record utilizing;

```
sudo service cups restart
```

Stage 4: User Access Settings

Next we add the Pi client to the Ipadmin gathering. This enables the Raspberry Pi to perform managerial elements of CUPS without fundamentally being a super client.

```
sudo usermod -a -G Ipadmin pi
```

Stage 5: Network Accessibility

Next we have to guarantee that CUPS can be associated with on the home system and its additionally open over the whole system.

To get it to permit all associations on the system, run;

```
sudo cupsctl –remote-any
```

After this we at that point restart cups to impact changes utilizing;

```
sudo /etc/init.d/cups restart
```

With this done we can continue to test in case it works adequately by looking at the CUPS landing page.

Open an internet browser as well as type in your Pi's IP address, showing the cups port.

e.g 192.168.137.147:631

631 is the cups port.

You should see the cups landing page like the picture beneath.

If you don't mind note that your program may caution you about the security testament of the site yet simply click on overlook and continue. Is that right?, I know, I had questions as well while attempting, yet haven't had any security break from that point forward so...

With this done we are prepared to move to the subsequent stage.

Stage 6: Setting Up Samba on Raspberry pi

Samba is an interoperability instrument that takes into consideration simple correspondence among windows and linux or unix projects and it will be utilized to permit our windows based framework to speak with CUPS running on the Raspberry Pi to print.

While cups is being introduced, it introduces different conditions like samba, however just in the event that it wasn't introduced, you can introduce it by following the strategy underneath.

Run:

```
sudo apt-get install samba
```

Trust that the establishment will run its course at

that point continue to arrange samba.

Stage 7: Configure Samba

Arrange samba by opening the setup document utilizing;

```
sudo nano /etc/samba/samba.conf
```

In the conf document, look to the print area and change the; visitor alright = no to visitor alright = yes

```
guest ok = yes
```

Additionally under the printer driver area, change the; read just = yes to peruse just = no

```
read only = no
```

With this all done spare the document utilizing ctrl +X pursued by y and enter.

Subsequent to sparing the document restart samba to impact the progressions utilizing;

```
sudo /etc/init.d/samba restart
```

With samba introduced, our Raspberry Pi is at long last fit to be connected to a printer so we make the last stride which is adding a printer to cups.

Adding a Printer to CUPS

Adding a printer to cups is formally one of the least demanding activity, go to the CUPS landing page again by entering your PI's IP address into an internet browser pursued by ":631" which is port location on which CUPS is conveying, your Pi's IP address can be gotten effectively by running the direction;

hostname –I

Presently on the landing page, click on the organization tab.

This will take you to the organization page where you

will see include new printer. Pursue the prompts, select your printer server and proceed.

On the last stage before tapping on proceed, guarantee you checked the "share this printer" check box.

With this you are altogether done, move the printer to the favored area, fire up your Raspberry Pi and print away.

Goodness before it slips my mind (racing to get some chicken, it's Christmas), to include the new made system printer on your Windows PC, go to gadgets and printers, select "Include a printer"

Snap on Next, Then select the printer I need isn't recorded on the following page

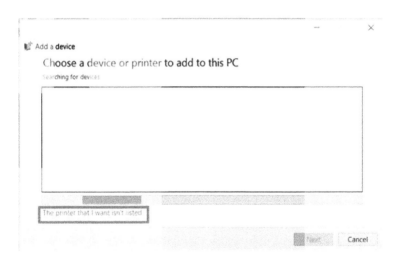

At that point enter the IP address of your PI pursued by the printer name on the following page utilizing the underneath position:

http://+ Raspberry Pi IP + :631 +/printers/+ your printer's name "Line Name" in CUPS

e.g http://192.168.137.147:631/printers/hp5XXX

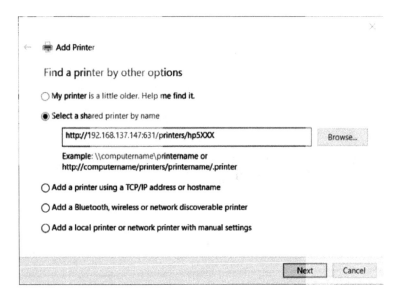

With this done, you should now have the option to print through a Raspberry Pi arrange printer.

That is it for this instructional exercise folks.

7. THE MOST EFFECTIVE METHOD TO INSTALL KODI ON RASPBERRY PI 3 RUNNING ON RASPBIAN

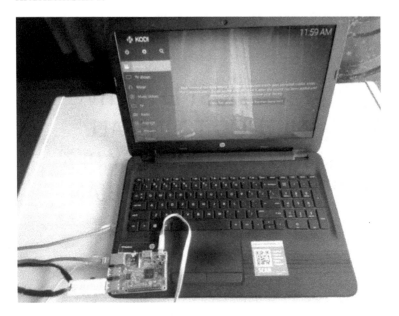

Hello there folks, we are in the soul of spilling and getting to media documents from anyplace and all over and that is the reason as a follow up to the last instructional exercise which is the execution of a Plex server on the Raspberry Pi, for this instructional exercise, we will actualize the KODI 17.4 (krypton) on our Raspberry Pi 3 running Raspbian Jessie.

Introduction to Kodi Media Player:

Kodi/XBMC is free as well as open source media player programming which can playback media records including sound, video and show pictures privately put away on a drive associated with the PC on which the product is running. It can likewise be used to stream recordings, sounds and pictures from the web. It is equipped for playing this media documents made in any of the mainstream record positions. KODI/XBMC is made to run in full screen mode and is in this way better when utilized with a TV screen however can likewise be utilized with a screen with a keypad or mouse for control/route of the KODI screen.

There are a few KODI prebuilt Operating framework for the Raspberry Pi like openELEC, RASPBMC, Xbian, yet when you utilize the Raspberry Pi for a million different things with various space necessities you would concur with me it's smarter to have it introduce on your preferred OS so you can deal with different things. For this instructional exercise of transforming your Raspberry pi into Media Server, we will introduce KODI on the Raspbian in light of the fact that it occupies less room on the Secure Digital card as well as its more advantageous to do different assignments than booting both Raspbian as well as a KODI based OS together.

Required Components:

For this venture, the accompanying segments will be required.

- Raspberry pi 3
- SD card (8gb at least)
- USB Drive or External Hard Disk
- HDMI Cable
- Display Monitor

For introducing Kodi/XBMC on Raspberry Pi, we are utilizing Raspberry Pi 3 with Raspbian Jessie OS. All the fundamental Hardware and Software prerequisites are recently talked about, you can find it in the Raspberry Pi Introduction.

So here I am accepting that you know about setting up the Raspberry Pi and you realize how to get to your Raspberry Pi by means of terminal utilizing programming like putty. Those are entirely fundamental stuffs which you can gain from our past Raspberry Pi ventures.

We will introduce Kodi on Raspbian in underneath steps, tail them cautiously and the venture will have exactly the intended effect. Gives jump access!

Installing Kodi Media Server on Raspberry Pi 3:

Stage 1: Upgrading the Pi

Its natural for me to refresh my raspberry pi before beginning any new venture and you ought to figure out how to do that as well. To refresh the pi, run;

```
sudo apt-get update

sudo apt-get upgrade
```

With this done, reboot the pi;

```
sudo reboot
```

Trust that the Pi will experience reboot then hop to stage 2

Stage 2: Adding Pipplware repo to Sources

The pipplware vault guarantee we generally have the present and stable arrival of KODI quicker than the official Raspberry Pi store, so we will introduce kodi from the pipplware repo and along these lines need to add the repo to the RPi sources list.

Pursue the means underneath to do this.

1.Add the pipplware repo to/and so forth/well-suited/sources.list utilizing;

```
sudo nano /etc/apt/sources.list
```

At the point when the record opens, include the accompanying line beneath it;

```
deb http://pipplware.pplware.pt/pipplware.dists/
jessie/main/binary /
```

Spare and leave utilizing CTRL +X then y

2.The following stage is to include the keys.

Attempt;

```
Wget –o – http://pipplware.pplware.pt/pipplware/
key.asc | sudo apt-key add –
```

This dealt with my first Raspberry Pi however I got the blunder underneath while attempting to reproduce and test again on another pi before posting the instructional exercise.

```
pi@raspberrypi:~ $ wget -o - http://pipplware.pplware.pt/pipplware/key.asc | sud
o apt-key add -
gpg: no valid OpenPGP data found.
pi@raspberrypi:~ $ ^C
pi@raspberrypi:~ $ ^C
pi@raspberrypi:~ $ wget --no-check-certificate -q -o - http://pipplware.pplware.
pt/pipplware/key.asc | sudo apt-key add -
gpg: no valid OpenPGP data found.
pi@raspberrypi:~ $ wget --no-check-certificate -q -o - http://pipplware.pplware.
pt/pipplware/key.asc
pi@raspberrypi:~ $ sudo apt-key add key.asc
OK
pi@raspberrypi:~ $
```

To comprehend this I incorporated a – no-registration and did a split of the direction.

So run;

wget –no-check-certificate –q –o – http://pipplware.pplware.pt/pipplware/key.asc

Pursued by;

sudo apt-key add key.asc

This must return OK then move to stage 3

3.After including the key, we at that point need to refresh the sources and overhaul the pi

To do this, run;

```
Sudo apt-get update && sudo apt-get dist-upgrade
```

At that point run a reboot.

With this done, we would then be able to go to stage 3.

Stage 3: KODI establishment and arrangement

Under this progression, we will introduce KODI and play out extra settings.

1.Install KODI. This should be possible utilizing;

```
sudo apt-get install kodi
```

2.We need to set a few authorizations for kodi. Run;

```
sudo addgroup --system input
```

3.The next thing is to make the info rules.

Make another record utilizing;

```
sudo nano /etc/udev/rules.d/99-input.rules
```

At that point include the lines underneath.

```
SUBSYSTEM==input, GROUP=input, MODE=0660

    KERNEL ==tty[0-9]*, GROUP =tty, MODE
=0660
```

4.Next we make the consents rules.

Make another document utilizing;

```
Sudo nano /etc/udev/rules.d/10-permissions.rules
```

At that point include the accompanying lines be-neath in the documents.

```
#input

KERNEL=="mouse|mice|event|",  MODE ="0660,
GROUP="input"

KERNEL=="ts[0-9]|uinput",          MODE="0660",
GROUP="input"

KERNEL==js[0-9], MODE=0660, GROUP=input

#tty

KERNEL==tty[0-9]*, MODE = 0666
```

```
#vchiq

SUBSYTEM==vchiq, GROUP=video, MODE=0660
```

Spare the document and exit.

5.We need to run the accompanying directions to perform different settings essential for kodi to run easily.

Simply pursue them one the other.

```
Sudo usermod –a –G audio pi

Sudo usermod – a –G video pi

Sudo usermod – a – G input pi

Sudo usermod – a –G dialout pi

Sudo usermod –a –G plugdev pi

Sudo usermod –a –G tty pi
```

With this means all done, we are prepared to begin utilizing Kodi.

Sympathetically note that the "pi" toward the finish of the directions is the client name. so in the event that you have altered the username of your raspberry pi, you should alter the pi to whatever your client name is.

Prior to propelling however, I will exhort you pursue a sudo reboot this stage.

Stage 4: Stream on!
Kodi can be either introduced to begin consequently with the raspberry pi boot or run it from the order window.

To run from the order window (which is favored by me, basically issue the direction;

```
kodi-standalone
```

This will dispatch kodi and you can see things by means of the screen.

To begin Kodi consequently on Boot, you should include a Kodi upstart content.

Run the accompanying direction to do that.

```
sudo wget –o /etc/init.d/kodi

https://gist.githubusercontent.com/shyam-
jos/60ea61fd8932fd5c868c80543b34f033/raw;
sudo chmod +x /etc/init.d/kodi
```

At that point empower the upstart content by running the direction beneath

```
sudo systemctl enable kodi
```

Should you ever need to debilitate the upstart content, run;

```
sudo systemctl disable kodi
```

This will incapacitate from running consequently at framework boot.

With this done you have effectively introduced Kodi on your raspberry pi.

Other Useful Commands for Kodi

To begin kodi from the terminal, then again you can

utilize;

```
sudo systemctl start kodi
```

To check the status of Kodi through terminal, run;

```
sudo systemctl status kodi
```

To prevent Kodi from running;

```
sudo systemctl stop kodi
```

Additional Info: Enabling shutdown/reboot Option in Power Menu

This progression tells the better way to include a shutdown or reboot choices to the Kodi control menu. To do this we will most importantly need to introduce policykit-1 at that point make another approach pack record.

Run;

```
sudo    nano    /etc/polkit-1/localauthority/50-
local.d/all_users_shutdown_reboot.pkla
```

At that point add the accompanying lines beneath to the document

```
Identity=unix-user:*

Action=org.freedesktop.login1.*;org.freedesk-
top.upower.*;org.freedesktop.consolekit.system.*

ResultActive=yes

ResultAny=yes

ResultInactive=yes
```

This will enable all clients to close down and reboot kodi from the Power menu.

That is it for this instructional exercise folks.

8. RASPBERRY PI BALL TRACKING ROBOT UTILIZING PROCESSING

The field of Robotics, Artificial Intelligence as well as Machine Learning is advancing quickly that it makes certain to change the way of life of humanity in not so distant future. Robots are thought to comprehend and communicate with this present reality through sensors and AI handling. Picture acknowledgment is one of the prominent manner by which the robots are thought to comprehend questions by taking a gander at this present reality through a camera simply as we do. In this venture, let utilize the intensity of Raspberry Pi to manufacture a Robot that could follow ball and tail it simply like the robots that plays football.

OpenCV is an extremely acclaimed and open source instrument that is utilized for Image handling, yet in this instructional exercise to keep things straightforward we are utilizing the Processing IDE. Since handling for ARM has likewise discharged the GPIO library for preparing we won't need to move among python and preparing any longer to work with Raspberry Pi. Sounds cool right? So let us begin.

Hardware Required:

- Raspberry Pi
- Robot Chassis
- Camera module with strip link
- Rigging engines with wheel
- Power bank or some other convenient power source
- L293D engine driver

Programming Requirement:

- Screen or other presentation for Raspberry pi
- Handling ARM programming
- Console otherwise mouse for Pi

Note: It is obligatory to have a presentation associated with Pi through wires during programming in light of the fact that at exactly that point the camera's video can be seen

Setting up Processing on Raspberry Pi:

As told before we will utilize the handling condition to Program our Raspberry Pi as well as not the default method for utilizing python. Thus, pursue the means beneath:

Stage 1:- Connect your Raspberry Pi to your screen, console and mouse and turn it on.

Stage 2:- Make sure you Pi is associated with a functioning web association since we are going to download not many things.

Stage 3:- Click on Processing ARM, to download the preparing IDE for Raspberry Pi. The download will be as a ZIP document.

Stage 4:- Once downloaded, remove the documents in your ZIP organizer in you favored catalog. I just separated it on my work area.

Stage 5:- Now, open the removed organizer and snap on the document named preparing. It should open a window as demonstrated as follows.

Stage 6:- This is nature where we will type our codes. For individuals who know about Arduino, don't be stunned YES the IDE looks like Arduino thus does the program.

Stage 7:- We need two libraries for our ball following system to work, to introduce then simply click on Sketch - > Import Library - > Add Library. The accompanying exchange box will open.

Stage 8:- Use the upper left content box to scan for Raspberry Pi and hit enter, you item should look something like this.

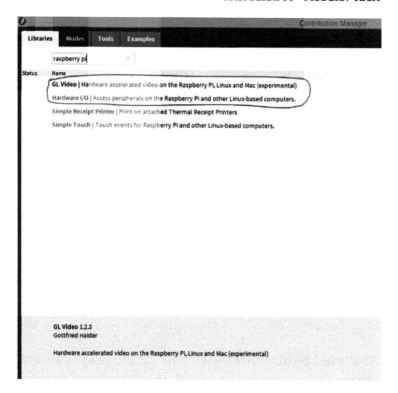

Stage 9:- Search for the libraries named "GL Video" and "Equipment I/O" and snap on introduce to introduce them. Ensure you introduce both the libraries.

Stage 10:- Based on your web the establishment will take few moments. When done we are prepared with for handling programming.

Circuit Diagram:

The circuit Diagram of this Raspberry Pi Ball Tracking Project is demonstrated as follows.

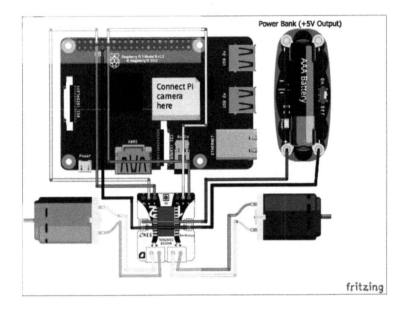

As should be obvious the circuit includes a PI camera, Motor Driver module as well as a couple of engines associated with the Raspberry pi. The total circuit is controlled by a Mobile Power bank (spoke to by AAA battery in the circuit above).

Since the pins subtleties are not referenced on the Raspberry Pi, we have to check the pins utilizing the beneath picture

To drive the Motors, we need four pins (A,B,A,B). This four pins are associated from GPIO 14,4,17 and 18 separately. The orange and white wire together structures the association for one engine. So we have two such matches for two engines.

The engines are associated with the L293D Motor Driver module as appeared in the image and the driver module is controlled by a power bank. Ensure that the ground of the power bank is associated with the ground of the Raspberry Pi, at exactly that point your association will work.

That is it we are finished with our Hardware association, how about we return to our handling condition and start programming to show our robot how to follow a ball.

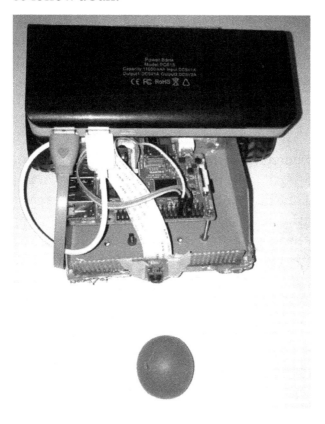

Raspberry Pi Ball tracking Program:

The total Processing system of this venture is given toward the finish of this page, which you legitimately use. Further just beneath, I have clarified the working of the code so you can utilize it for other comparative ventures.

The program idea is exceptionally straightforward. In spite of the fact that the expectation of the venture is to follow a ball, we are really not going to do it. We are simply going to recognize the ball utilizing its shading. As we as a whole realize recordings are only consistent casings of pictures. So we snap every photo as well as split it into pixels. At that point we contrast every pixel shading and the shade of the ball; on the off chance that a match is discovered, at that point we can say that we have discovered the ball. With this data we can likewise recognize the situation of the ball (pixel shading) on the screen. In the event that the position is far left we move the robot to right, if the position is far right we move the robot to left with the goal that the pixel position consistently remains at the focal point of the screen. You can watch Computer Vision video of Daniel shiffman to get an unmistakable picture.

As consistently we start by bringing in the two libraries that we download. This should be possible by the accompanying two lines. The Hardware I/O library is utilized to get to the GPIO pins of the PI legitimately from the preparing condition, the glvideo library is utilized to get to the Raspberry Pi camera module.

```
import processing.io.*;

import gohai.glvideo.*;
```

Inside the arrangement work we instate the yield pins to control the engine and furthermore get the video from the pi camera and size it in a window of size 320 * 240.

```
void setup() {

  size(320, 240, P2D);

  video = new GLCapture(this);

  video.start();

  trackColor = color(255, 0, 0);

  GPIO.pinMode(4, GPIO.OUTPUT);

  GPIO.pinMode(14, GPIO.OUTPUT);

  GPIO.pinMode(17, GPIO.OUTPUT);
```

```
GPIO.pinMode(18, GPIO.OUTPUT);

}
```

The void draw resembles the interminable circle the code inside this circle will be execute as long as the program is ended. In the event that a camera source is accessible we perused the video leaving it

```
void draw() {

  background(0);

  if(video.available()) {

    video.read();

}}
```

At that point we start to part the video outline into pixels. Every pixel has an estimation of red, green as well as blue. These qualities are put away in the variable r1, g1 and b1

```
for (int x = 0; x < video.width; x ++ ) {

  for (int y = 0; y < video.height; y ++ ) {
```

```
int loc = x + y*video.width;

// What is current color

color currentColor = video.pixels[loc];

float r1 = red(currentColor);

float g1 = green(currentColor);

float b1 = blue(currentColor);
```

To recognize the shade of the ball at first, we require to tap on the shading. When click the shade of the ball will be put away in factor called trackColour.

```
void mousePressed() {

  // Save color where the mouse is clicked in track-
  Color variable

  int loc = mouseX + mouseY*video.width;

  trackColor = video.pixels[loc];

}
```

When we have the track shading and the present shading we need to look at them. This examination is utilizing the dist work. It checks how close the present shading is to the track shading.

```
float d = dist(r1, g1, b1, r2, g2, b2);
```

The estimation of dist will be zero for a definite match. Along these lines, if the estimation of dist is not exactly a predefined esteem (world Record) at that point we expect that we have discovered the track shading. At that point we get the area of that pixel and store it in the variable nearest X and nearest Y to discover the area of the ball

```
if(d < worldRecord){

    worldRecord = d;

    closestX = x;

    closestY = y;

}
```

We additionally draw a circle around the discovered shading to show that the shading has been found. The estimation of the position is likewise imprinted on the support, this will support a great deal while troubleshooting.

```
if(worldRecord < 10){

   // Draw a circle at the tracked pixel

   fill(trackColor);

   strokeWeight(4.0);

   stroke(0);

   ellipse(closestX, closestY, 16, 16);

   println(closestX,closestY);
```

At last we can look at the situation of the nearest X and nearest Y and modify the engines so that the shading gets to the focal point of the screen. The underneath code is utilized to turn the robot directly since the X position of the shading was seen as in the left half of the screen (<140)

```
if(closestX<140)

   {

   GPIO.digitalWrite(4, GPIO.HIGH);
```

```
    GPIO.digitalWrite(14, GPIO.HIGH);

    GPIO.digitalWrite(17, GPIO.HIGH);

    GPIO.digitalWrite(18, GPIO.LOW);

    delay(10);

    GPIO.digitalWrite(4, GPIO.HIGH);

    GPIO.digitalWrite(14, GPIO.HIGH);

    GPIO.digitalWrite(17, GPIO.HIGH);

    GPIO.digitalWrite(18, GPIO.HIGH);

    println("Turn Right");

}
```

So also we can check the situation of X and Y to control the engines in the necessary course. As consistently you can allude the base of the page for the total program.

Working of Raspberry Pi Ball Tracking Robot:

When you are prepared with the equipment and program it's an ideal opportunity to have a ton of fun. Before we test our bot on ground, we should ensure everything is working fine. Associate your Pi to screen and dispatch the handling code. You should see the video feed on a little window. Presently, bring the ball inside the casing and snap on the ball to show the robot that it should follow this specific shading. Presently move the ball around the screen and you should see the wheels pivoting.

In the event that everything is filling in true to form, discharge the bot on the ground and began playing with it. Ensure the room is equitably lit up for best outcomes. Expectation you comprehended the undertaking and appreciated structure something comparable.

Code

```
/*
Processing Raspberry Pi program for Ball following
Robot

#This project would not have been possible without
the help of Daniel Shiffman and Gottfried Haider
*/
import processing.io.*;
import gohai.glvideo.*;
GLCapture video;
color trackColor;
void setup() {
 size(320, 240, P2D);
 video = new GLCapture(this);
 video.start();


  trackColor = color(255, 0, 0);


  GPIO.pinMode(4, GPIO.OUTPUT);
 GPIO.pinMode(14, GPIO.OUTPUT);
 GPIO.pinMode(17, GPIO.OUTPUT);
 GPIO.pinMode(18, GPIO.OUTPUT);
}
void draw() {
 background(0);
 if (video.available()) {
  video.read();
 }
```

```
 video.loadPixels();
image(video, 0, 0);


 float worldRecord = 500;
int closestX = 0;
int closestY = 0;


 // Begin loop to walk through every pixel
for (int x = 0; x < video.width; x ++ ) {
 for (int y = 0; y < video.height; y ++ ) {
  int loc = x + y*video.width;
  // What is current color
  color currentColor = video.pixels[loc];
  float r1 = red(currentColor);
  float g1 = green(currentColor);
  float b1 = blue(currentColor);
  float r2 = red(trackColor);
  float g2 = green(trackColor);
  float b2 = blue(trackColor);
  // Using euclidean distance to compare colors
   float d = dist(r1, g1, b1, r2, g2, b2); // We are using
the dist( ) function to compare the current color with
the color we are tracking.

   // If current color is more similar to tracked color
than
   // closest color, save current location and current
difference
  if (d < worldRecord) {
```

```
  worldRecord = d;
  closestX = x;
  closestY = y;
 }
 }
}


if (worldRecord < 10) {
// Draw a circle at the tracked pixel
fill(trackColor);
strokeWeight(4.0);
stroke(0);
ellipse(closestX, closestY, 16, 16);
println(closestX,closestY);


  if (closestX<140)
{
GPIO.digitalWrite(4, GPIO.HIGH);
GPIO.digitalWrite(14, GPIO.HIGH);
GPIO.digitalWrite(17, GPIO.HIGH);
GPIO.digitalWrite(18, GPIO.LOW);
delay(10);
GPIO.digitalWrite(4, GPIO.HIGH);
GPIO.digitalWrite(14, GPIO.HIGH);
GPIO.digitalWrite(17, GPIO.HIGH);
GPIO.digitalWrite(18, GPIO.HIGH);


  println("Turn Right");
}
```

```
else if (closestX>200)
{
GPIO.digitalWrite(4, GPIO.HIGH);
GPIO.digitalWrite(14, GPIO.LOW);
GPIO.digitalWrite(17, GPIO.HIGH);
GPIO.digitalWrite(18, GPIO.HIGH);
delay(10);
GPIO.digitalWrite(4, GPIO.HIGH);
GPIO.digitalWrite(14, GPIO.HIGH);
GPIO.digitalWrite(17, GPIO.HIGH);
GPIO.digitalWrite(18, GPIO.HIGH);
println("Turn Left");
}
else if (closestY<170)
{
GPIO.digitalWrite(4, GPIO.HIGH);
GPIO.digitalWrite(14, GPIO.LOW);
GPIO.digitalWrite(17, GPIO.HIGH);
GPIO.digitalWrite(18, GPIO.LOW);
delay(10);
GPIO.digitalWrite(4, GPIO.HIGH);
GPIO.digitalWrite(14, GPIO.HIGH);
GPIO.digitalWrite(17, GPIO.HIGH);
GPIO.digitalWrite(18, GPIO.HIGH);
println("Go Frwd");
}
else
{
GPIO.digitalWrite(4, GPIO.HIGH);
GPIO.digitalWrite(14, GPIO.HIGH);
```

```
 GPIO.digitalWrite(17, GPIO.HIGH);
 GPIO.digitalWrite(18, GPIO.HIGH);
  }
 }
 else
 {
  GPIO.digitalWrite(4, GPIO.HIGH);
  GPIO.digitalWrite(14, GPIO.HIGH);
  GPIO.digitalWrite(17, GPIO.HIGH);
  GPIO.digitalWrite(18, GPIO.HIGH);
 }
}
void mousePressed() {
  // Save color where the mouse is clicked in track-
Color variable
 int loc = mouseX + mouseY*video.width;
 trackColor = video.pixels[loc];
}
```

❖ ❖ ❖

9. INSTRUCTIONS TO SET UP PLEX MEDIA SERVER ON RASPBERRY PI

Greetings folks, so one of the issues with the computerized age is having so a lot of information put
away to a large extent, particularly media records, its
constantly an agony when you have that main tune
on your PC at home and you can't generally get to it
or offer with few other individual from some other
piece of the house except if you come down to where
its found. The entirety of this specific sort of issues
and other comparable ones are what Plex attempted
to comprehend and for this instructional exercise,
we will introduce the Plex server on your Raspberry
Pi, giving you boundless, not fastened availability to
your media library.

Introduction to Plex Server:

Plex is a customer server media player framework, which has a Plex Server to serve every one of the media documents and a Plex Client to access or stream every one of the media records from the server.

1. The Plex Media Server can be run on many Operating Systems like Windows, macOS as well as Linux and so forth. Plex arrange all you media records, regardless of whether it be music, motion pictures, photographs, appears, in clean way with blurbs and thumbnails and furthermore show evaluations and different things from the online administrations. Here we are utilizing Raspberry Pi as Plex Server.

2. Media players are the customers running on the customer gadgets like versatile, PC and so forth. Customers can get to the media records from the Plex Server.

The Plex Home Media Server enables you to keep every one of your media records in a single spot and access them from any of your different gadgets. You can get to the information from all your preferred gadgets like Web, Android Smart telephone, Apple, Amazon fire TV, iOS, Windows, Xbox, PlayStation, Chromecast, Smart TVs and so forth. Plex Client is bolstered for these gadgets.

For this instructional exercise, we will make the Plex server on Rasbperry Pi. You will have the option to transfer your media documents to the joined stockpiling (USB pen drive or External HD) and afterward stream the media from the server to some other gadget, be it cell phone, or associated PC. This could be a valuable instrument as it encourages you deal with the space on the entirety of your different gadgets very well and makes offering to loved ones simple.

Required Components:

- Raspberry Pi 3 (should work fine with Pi 2)
- USB Drive or External Hard disk (Optional)
- Secure Digital card (at least 8 GigaByte)

In this raspberry pi plex server instructional exercise we are utilizing Raspberry Pi 3 with Raspbian Jessie OS. All the fundamental Hardware and Software prerequisites are recently examined, you can find it in the Raspberry Pi Introduction.

So here I am accepting that you know about setting up the Raspberry Pi and you realize how to get to your Raspberry Pi through terminal utilizing programming like putty. Part of presumptions right? Yea however those are entirely fundamental stuffs which you can gain from our past Raspberry Pi ventures.

We will take executing the Plex server on Raspberry Pi in steps, tail them cautiously and the task will have exactly the intended effect. Gives jump access!

Setting up Plex Server on Raspberry Pi:

Stage 1: Upgrading the Pi

The primary thing I like doing before beginning each undertaking is refreshing the pi, to get each most recent update to the OS in. we do that utilizing;

```
sudo apt-get update

sudo apt-get upgrade
```

With this done, reboot the pi utilizing;

```
sudo reboot
```

Sit tight for some time, at that point restart the terminal session and keep on venturing 2.

Stage 2: Static IP Address for the Pi

The following thing we have to do is to relegate a static IP address to our raspberry pi.

Initially thing we have to do is make certain of the present IP address. This should be possible utilizing;

```
sudo hostname -I
```

This will show the present IP address. Duplicate and be careful.

Next, we alter the cmdline.txt document of the raspberry pi to incorporate the IP address.

sudo nano /boot/cmdline.txt

Include the beneath line toward the finish of the document, supplant "IP_ADDRESS" with your IP address"

ip=IP_ADDRESS

Reboot the raspberry pi to impact changes.

sudo reboot

Stage 3: Install HTTPS transport bundle

Next thing for us is to introduce (or affirm that we have introduced) the HTTPS transport. This however accompanies more up to date form of the raspbian and its should have been ready to get to the https bundles by means of well-suited get.

```
sudo apt-get install apt-transport-https
```

This will introduce the most recent adaptation. In the event that you as of now have it, you'll simply recover a message kicked letting you know so. In any case, you're currently prepared for the subsequent stage.

Stage 4: Get the dev2day archive

The following thing we have to do is get the dev2day storehouse (A task documentation on plex) which contains Plex however to do this we need a sepulcher O key for the dev2day site.

To get the tomb O key;

```
wget  -O  -  https://dev2day.de/pms/dev2day-
pms.gpg.key | sudo apt-key add -
```

dont overlook the – toward the end.

You may experience an issue at this phase where the terminal will return something like this;

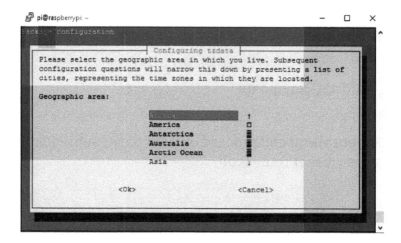

This issue is related with your pi making some off-base memories and date. To fix this, run;

sudo dpkg-reconfigure tzdata

At that point select your timezone, and nearest city

At that point utilize the line showed underneath to set the specific time.

```
pi@raspberrypi:~ $ sudo date -s "Oct 22 11:40"
Sun 22 Oct 11:40:00 WAT 2017
pi@raspberrypi:~ $ sudo reboot
login as: pi
pi@raspberrypi.mshome.net's password:
```

Reboot the Pi and run the direction to get the sepulcher 0 key once more.

All done? Next, we'll add dev2day's vault to the bundle source list.

echo "deb https://dev2day.de/pms/ jessie main " | sudo tee /etc/apt/sources.list.d/pms.list

It will simply restore a line with the reverberated information.

At last, update the bundle list utilizing;

sudo apt-get update

Reboot the pi and proceed onward to the subsequent stage when it returns on.

sudo reboot

Stage 5: Install Plex Media Server

With the gadget back on, we are at last prepared to introduce Plex!. To do this we utilize the order;

```
sudo apt-get install -t jessie plexmediaserver
```

Answer yes (by squeezing y) in the event that it requests your authorization to introduce any reliance.

Stage 6: Setup Plex to run on the 'Pi' client

Next thing we have to do is arrangement Plex to run on the 'Pi' client with which we are signed in. To do this, we have to alter the plexmediaserver.prev record and change the client from plex to pi. To do this we use

```
sudo nano /etc/default/plexmediaserver.prev
```

This will open up a book document. We are searching for the piece of the content record that says

```
PLEX_MEDIA_SERVER_USER=plex
```

We will transform it so it becomes;

```
PLEX_MEDIA_SERVER_USER=pi.
```

```
pi@raspberrypi: ~                                        —    □

 GNU nano 2.2.6        File: /etc/default/plexmediaserver.prev

PLEX_MEDIA_SERVER_TMPDIR=/tmp

# uncomment to set it to something else
# PLEX_MEDIA_SERVER_APPLICATION_SUPPORT_DIR="${HOME}/Library/Application\ Sup

# the user that PMS should run as, defaults to 'plex'
# note that if you change this you might need to move
# the Application Support directory to not lose your
# media library
PLEX_MEDIA_SERVER_USER=plex
```

Spare the content document as regular and leave utilizing CTRL+X and afterward y.

With this done, restart your plex server to impact changes utilizing;

```
sudo service plexmediaserver restart
```

with this done, reboot your pi by and by as we impact the last changes.

```
sudo reboot
```

That is it folks, we have Plex server all set ready for action on our Raspberry Pi, yet i'd state the server is pointless on the off chance that we don't stack records on it right? So the following hardly any means will be tied in with telling us the best way to stack documents in and furthermore stream the records from associated gadgets.

Stage 7: Upload the records on Plex Server

The progression will tell you the best way to populate your Plex media server.

The primary thing is to associate a usb drive or an outer hard circle containing the media documents with which you need to populate the server to your Pi.

With this done, we open an internet browser as well as go to;

MyPiIPAdress:32400/web/

Otherwise on the other hand

raspberrypi.mshome.net:32400/web/

This will carry you to the plex web application, sign in or make a record.

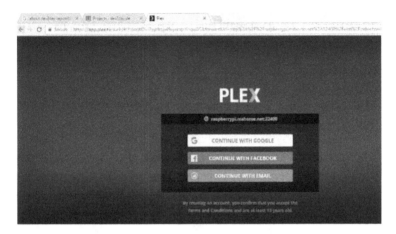

Plex will give you how things work and you will perceive how to include library. Explore through your envelope, select the right kind of record and add them to your Plex library.

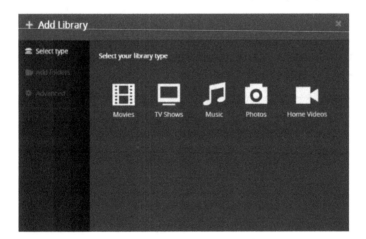

That is everything, you can now effectively interface any customer gadget on a similar system, and Plex will associate it to your server.

Stage 7: Access the records from Plex Client

To do this you should introduce and open the Plex application from a customer gadget and in the event that they are on a similar system, it will have exactly the intended effect. As referenced as of now Plex Client can be in any way similar to your Mobile Phone, Computer, Smart TV, Playstation and so on.

That is it folks.

10. CONTROLLING RASPBERRY PI GPIO PINS UTILIZING TELEGRAM APP

Message is an ideal application to consolidate with Raspberry Pi for all our versatile control reason. It has awesome engineer backing and heaps of highlights are being wanted to be discharged soon to upgrade the exhibition of Telegram Bots. In our past instructional exercise we figured out how we can arrange up a wire bot for raspberry pi and furthermore learnt must have a talk with it and offer pictures, reports and Audio documents.

Presently, we will continue to following stage by figuring out How we can control the GPIO nails to Raspberry Pins utilizing Telegram, with the goal that we give some equipment backing to our bot. In this instructional exercise we will Connect four LEDs to Raspberry Pi GPIO pins and switch them utilizing common language (visiting like) from Telegram. Sounds fascinating right? Give us a opportunity to begin.

Materials Required:

- Four LED (any color)
- Breadboard
- Raspberry Pi (with internet connection)
- Connecting wires

Pre-Requisites:

Before continuing with the instructional exercise ensure your Raspberry Pi is associated with web and you can run python programs on your Pi. Additionally read the past instructional exercise to realize how to set up Telegram bot with Raspberry Pi, since I will expect you know about that stuff to continue with the undertaking.

In the event that you are new to Raspberry Pi, at that point pursue our Raspberry Pi Introduction article and other Raspberry Pi Tutorials.

Circuit Diagram:

The circuit Diagram for managing Light Emitting Diodes utilizing Raspberry Pi as well as Telegram Android Application is simply 4 Light Emitting Diodes as well as few interfacing wires. We won't require the present constraining resistors since the Raspberry Pi GPIO pins take a shot at 3.3V TTL. Pursue the circuit underneath and associate your LED.

The accompanying table will assist you with deciding the pin number and GPIO number for the association of four leds.

Led Terminal	Pin Number	GPIO Number
Green Anode	Pin 31	GPIO 6
Red Anode	Pin 33	GPIO 13
Yellow Anode	Pin 35	GPIO 19
White Anode	Pin 37	GPIO 26
Cathode of all four	Pin 39	Ground

The following is the Circuit outline in which four LEDs are associated by the Table given previously:

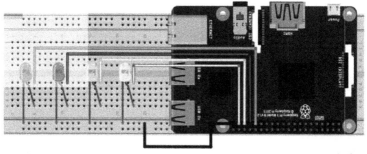

fritzing

When your associations your equipment set-up should look like something like this underneath.

Raspberry Python Program:

When the equipment is prepared, we can continue with the Python Program. In this program we need to peruse the information (message) sent from the Telegram bot and flip the LED likewise. To make it increasingly characteristic, rather than checking each sentence and hard coding those sentence inside our program we can check for words and continue as needs be.

So the program will essentially check for two words, they are on and off. When recognizing both of these 2 words, it will search for different watchwords like white, yellow, green and red. The particular shading LED will be flipped just if the word is recognized.

We will likewise refresh a string for the distinguished words to communicate something specific back to wire bot.

The total program can be found at the base of this page; just underneath I have clarified the program by breaking it into little significant throws out.

For this program to work, we require the telepot installed as well as imported in our Raspberry Pi. In our past instructional exercise we have just downloaded the transport inside our Raspberry Pi, so now we simply need to bring it into our program alongside the GPIO library as demonstrated as follows.

```
import RPi.GPIO as GPIO

import telepot

from telepot.loop import MessageLoop
```

We will control for LED lights utilizing this program and the shade of the LEDs will be White, Yellow, Red and Green. They are associated with the pins appeared in circuit graph; let us characterize the pin names for these LEDs dependent on their shading so it is use them in the program.

```
white = 26
```

```
yellow = 19

red = 13

green = 6
```

The following stage is characterize all these LED pins as yield sticks and characterize them as killed obviously by utilizing the beneath lines.

```
#LED White

GPIO.setup(white, GPIO.OUT)

GPIO.output(white, 0) #Off initially

#LED Yellow

GPIO.setup(yellow, GPIO.OUT)

GPIO.output(yellow, 0) #Off initially

#LED Red

GPIO.setup(red, GPIO.OUT)

GPIO.output(red, 0) #Off initially

#LED green
```

```
GPIO.setup(green, GPIO.OUT)

GPIO.output(green, 0) #Off initially
```

As we learnt in our past instructional exercise every one of the activities that must be finished by the Raspberry bot will be characterized inside the capacity activity. Here we need to cause the bot to tune in to the message to send from versatile, contrast it with certain catchphrases and switch LED likewise.

For each message we send from versatile, there will be a visit id and order. This talk id is required by the program to answer back to the sender. So we spare the talk id and, message as demonstrated as follows.

```
chat_id = msg['chat']['id']

command = msg['text']
```

Presently, whatever we send from the telephone will be spared as string in the variable direction. In this way, we should simply check for catchphrases in this factor. Python has a direction make things simple here. For instance, on the off chance that we need to check if "on" is available in the string put away in order variable we can basically utilize the beneath line.

```
if 'on' in command:
```

Correspondingly we check for all watchwords, when we get an "on", we continue to check for which shading the client has referenced. This is additionally done by similar directions by looking at similar catchphrases. We additionally update a string named message that can be answered back to the client as a status message.

```
if 'on' in command:

    message = "Turned on"

    if 'white' in command:

        message = message + "white "

        GPIO.output(white, 1)

    if 'yellow' in command:

        message = message + "yellow "

        GPIO.output(yellow, 1)

    if 'red' in command:
```

```
        message = message + "red "

        GPIO.output(red, 1)

    if 'green' in command:

        message = message + "green "

        GPIO.output(green, 1)

    if 'all' in command:

        message = message + "all "

        GPIO.output(white, 1)

        GPIO.output(yellow, 1)

        GPIO.output(red, 1)

        GPIO.output(green, 1)

    message = message + "light(s)"

    telegram_bot.sendMessage (chat_id, message)
```

As appeared above we search for catchphrases like 'green', 'white', 'red', 'yellow' and 'all' and 'Turned on' that specific LED alone. When the activity is done we communicate something specific back to the client about what simply occurred. A similar technique can be utilized to kill the lights off well.

```
if 'off' in command:

    message = "Turned off"

    if 'white' in command:

        message = message + "white "

        GPIO.output(white, 0)

    if 'yellow' in command:

        message = message + "yellow "

        GPIO.output(yellow, 0)

    if 'red' in command:

        message = message + "red "

        GPIO.output(red, 0)

    if 'green' in command:

        message = message + "green"
```

```
        GPIO.output(green, 0)

    if 'all' in command:

        message = message + "all "

        GPIO.output(white, 0)

        GPIO.output(yellow, 0)

        GPIO.output(red, 0)

        GPIO.output(green, 0)

    message = message + "light(s)"

    telegram_bot.sendMessage (chat_id, message)
```

Controlling LEDs with Raspberry Pi and Telegram bot:

Interface your LEDs and dispatch your program on python. Ensure you have changed the Token location for your bot. Furthermore, start composing in the directions you wish. For instance to turn on the red and yellow light you can utilize any of the accompanying order.

1.Turn on Red as well as Yellow Light

2.Switch on Red as well as Yellow shading right

3.On red as well as yellow

4.Please put on the yellow as well as red light

What not.......

As should be obvious the bot searches for the Keywords and will disregard different words in the Sentence, along these lines you can address it normally.

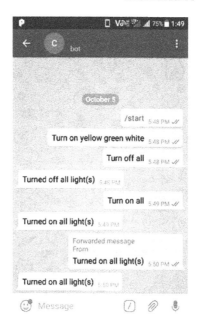

Proceed! play with your extend and have a great time. You can take it to an unheard of level at this point. With both the instructional exercise joined we have the ability to control any equipment from our Smart telephone anyplace from the world and furthermore get inputs/results from our Raspberry Pi in type of message, Audio, Image and even as record. In case you supplant the LEDs with Relays and AC apparatuses, at that point it could be a Smart Phone controlled Home Automation. Along these lines, utilize your imagination and manufacture your own cool undertakings...

Expectation you preferred the venture and appreciated structure something comparative. Fill me in as to whether you have any issues through the remark area and I will be glad to support you. Additionally share your cool thought with me and let us see what we can construct.

Code

```
import time, datetime
import RPi.GPIO as GPIO
import telepot
from telepot.loop import MessageLoop
white = 26
yellow = 19
red = 13
green = 6
now = datetime.datetime.now()
GPIO.setmode(GPIO.BCM)
GPIO.setwarnings(False)


#LED White
GPIO.setup(white, GPIO.OUT)
GPIO.output(white, 0) #Off initially
#LED Yellow
GPIO.setup(yellow, GPIO.OUT)
GPIO.output(yellow, 0) #Off initially
 #LED Red
GPIO.setup(red, GPIO.OUT)
GPIO.output(red, 0) #Off initially
#LED green
GPIO.setup(green, GPIO.OUT)
```

```
GPIO.output(green, 0) #Off initially
def action(msg):
  chat_id = msg['chat']['id']
  command = msg['text']
  print 'Received: %s' % command
  if 'on' in command:
    message = "Turned on "
    if 'white' in command:
      message = message + "white "
      GPIO.output(white, 1)
    if 'yellow' in command:
      message = message + "yellow "
      GPIO.output(yellow, 1)
    if 'red' in command:
      message = message + "red "
      GPIO.output(red, 1)
    if 'green' in command:
      message = message + "green "
      GPIO.output(green, 1)
    if 'all' in command:
      message = message + "all "
      GPIO.output(white, 1)
      GPIO.output(yellow, 1)
      GPIO.output(red, 1)
      GPIO.output(green, 1)
    message = message + "light(s)"
    telegram_bot.sendMessage (chat_id, message)
  if 'off' in command:
    message = "Turned off "
    if 'white' in command:
```

```
      message = message + "white "
      GPIO.output(white, 0)
    if 'yellow' in command:
      message = message + "yellow "
      GPIO.output(yellow, 0)
    if 'red' in command:
      message = message + "red "
      GPIO.output(red, 0)
    if 'green' in command:
      message = message + "green "
      GPIO.output(green, 0)
    if 'all' in command:
      message = message + "all "
      GPIO.output(white, 0)
      GPIO.output(yellow, 0)
      GPIO.output(red, 0)
      GPIO.output(green, 0)
    message = message + "light(s)"
    telegram_bot.sendMessage (chat_id, message)
telegram_bot = telepot.Bot('470583174:AAG7MP-
Zc93qchp-tjqA_K2meRYcQiOR7X7Y')
print (telegram_bot.getMe())
MessageLoop(telegram_bot, action).run_as_thread()
print 'Up and Running....'
while 1:
  time.sleep(10)
```

Thank You !!!